PRINCE
ANDREW

DONALD EDGAR

PRINCE ANDREW

ARTHUR BARKER LIMITED · LONDON
A subsidiary of Weidenfeld (Publishers) Limited

ISBN 0 213 16750 6

Set, printed and bound in Great Britain by
Fakenham Press Limited, Fakenham, Norfolk

Contents

Acknowledgments

I wish to thank Mr John King, Chief Librarian of the *Daily Express*, and his staff, who were once more most helpful, making available their comprehensive archives. The librarians at Canada House, London, were very co-operative. I would like to express my gratitude to the staff of the Chelsea Library, including the Reference Section, who have over the years given so much assistance to me on many subjects.

For certain historical references I have re-read with pleasure and profit Roger Fulford's *Royal Dukes, Queen Victoria's Wicked Uncles* (Gerald Duckworth, 1933, Pan Books, 1948) and A. Cecil Hampshire's *Royal Sailors* (Kimber, 1971).

My wife, Rosalie, has been unfailingly helpful in discussing the subject at all stages.

I am indebted to Mr Simon Dally, Managing Director of Arthur Barker Limited, for his encouragement and understanding.

For the views expressed I am responsible.

Donald Edgar
London, 1980

To my friend
Bernard Gibbs

I

A Matter of Seconds

Prince Andrew is the second son of the Queen and so stands next in line to the throne after his elder brother, Charles, Prince of Wales. The most likely course of events is that Charles will marry and his children, whether male or female, will take precedence over Andrew. His seniority in the line of succession will diminish with the birth of each child.

There are, nevertheless, eventualities which, far from diminishing, would enhance Andrew's importance and bring him even closer to the throne than he now is.

The most calamitous would be if Charles died young, before he had married and had a chance to have a family. Another possibility is that he marries, but for one reason or another there are no children. Then again he might decide not to get married at all.

There are also other possibilities which are peculiar to Charles's position. For example, if he marries a Roman Catholic he automatically loses his rights to the throne under an act of 1689 which established the Protestant succession. Then again he might wish to renounce his rights for personal reasons, such as a determination to marry a woman against the Queen's wishes, for she has the right to refuse approval under the terms of the Royal Marriage Act of 1772. Lastly, Charles needs no reminding that the British Government must also approve of his choice of bride, for his great-uncle, Edward VIII (later Duke of Windsor), was forced to abdicate by the British Government in 1936 because it disapproved of the woman he was resolved to marry, Mrs Wallis Simpson, an American who had twice been through the divorce courts.

Any of these regrettable eventualities could make Andrew heir to the throne and, perhaps, king. There have been stories from time to time that the Queen, aware of the uncertainties of life, has been treating Andrew in recent years as an understudy to Charles, but it is difficult to see any tangible evidence of this. It cannot be said that Andrew has been given much limelight as he has grown into his late teens. He has attracted some, but that is because he is a forceful and engaging young man.

However, if Andrew came to the throne, it would not be without precedent. In the course of the last five hundred years several second sons and daughters have reigned in England and it is a fascinating pastime to reflect how their accession to the British crown has influenced the history, not just of England, but also of Europe and even of the world as a whole.

One such second son was the redoubtable Henry viii. His elder brother was Prince Arthur, born in September 1486, the first child of the marriage of King Henry vii and Princess Elizabeth of York, daughter of Edward iv. The marriage was a unifying symbol of the end of the Wars of the Roses which had been fought between the House of Lancaster and York for the rule of England. Fortunately for England the casualties in the battles had for the most part been confined to the Norman and French aristocracy and their retainers. The future Henry vii commanded the army of Lancaster at the battle of Bosworth in 1485 which resulted in the defeat and death of Richard iii of the House of York. But the Houses of Lancaster and York were not destined to rule again, for Henry was by birth a Tudor with only tenuous family links with the Lancastrians. He came to the throne as the first king of the remarkable House of Tudor.

Henry was well aware of his shaky claim to the throne and when his first son was born determined to make the most of the event to consolidate his position. Although immensely close-fisted he ordered the birth to be celebrated with considerable magnificence. The child was named Arthur to recall the legendary British hero and to presage the rebirth of national glory. It was also a reminder to the nation that the Tudors were Welsh and that King Arthur had been a Celt who had flourished long before the English tribes came from Germany.

It was soon apparent that the boy was not strong, but it was hoped that care and a good diet would improve his health. The scope of education was widening as the Renaissance began to influence England; Arthur's mentors taught him Greek as well as Latin.

From the time Arthur was two years old, Henry vii was looking around for a future bride who would enhance the prestige of the dynasty and bring a rich dowry. He seemed fortunate in his search. Spain had become a united country following the marriage of Ferdinand of Aragon with Isabella of Castile, one of the ablest women in European history. Under their leadership Spain was entering a period of expansion which was to make it a world power. One of their daughters was Katharine of Aragon, a gentle girl, rather plain, grave in the Spanish fashion and a devoted daughter of the Church. Henry managed to secure her as a bride for Arthur with a handsome dowry. It was a political and financial coup.

Prince Arthur was fifteen and Katharine sixteen when they were married in St Paul's Cathedral on 14 November 1501. The King sent the young couple in late

December to Ludlow in the Welsh Marches to hold court. But Arthur's health deteriorated during the winter and on 2 April 1502 he died. There now seems little doubt that the marriage was not consummated, leaving Katharine a virgin widow.

It was a blow to Henry dynastically, politically and financially. Katharine's parents asked for her to be returned to Spain with the first instalment of the dowry which had been paid. Henry did not comply with either request. Then a Spanish ambassador was sent to suggest that Katharine should be married to Prince Henry, the new heir to the throne, when he was fourteen in 1505. Henry VII seemed to agree to this project and a dispensation was sought from the pope to enable young Henry to marry his brother's widow. This was obtained from Rome in 1504, probably due to the influence of Queen Isabella. By now Katharine's condition was deplorable. She had been forced to run into debt to buy the necessities of life and was treated as an outcast. Then the King became a widower and Isabella heard with horror that there were rumours that he intended to marry his daughter-in-law himself. Prince Henry's fourteenth birthday came and passed with no sign of the marriage to Katharine taking place. By this time the King was involved in a long, acrimonious squabble with Ferdinand and Isabella about the second instalment of the dowry.

Henry VII died in 1509 and was succeeded by his son as Henry VIII. He must have had some affection for Katharine as seven weeks later, in June of the same year, he married her. Henry was eighteen and Katharine twenty-four, having been a widow for seven years. In the early years of the marriage he seemed a devoted and loving husband.

Henry in those days was the embodiment of the Renaissance prince – handsome, vigorous, able, well-read and musical, with already a touch of ruthlessness. Katharine had several miscarriages, bore a daughter, Mary, who was to be queen, but no son to strengthen the dynasty. Henry, in his lusty fashion, enjoyed the favours of what women he fancied and fathered a son. By 1526, when the marriage had lasted seventeen years, Katharine had lost what looks she had possessed and at nearly forty-one was past child-bearing. There was already talk of a divorce to enable the King to marry a younger woman who might give him a son.

Then Henry fell in love with Anne Boleyn who seems, with well-nigh incredible skill, to have held the King at bay until she was sure of marrying him. In 1527 Henry asked Pope Clement VII for a divorce and in normal circumstances there can be little doubt that his request would have been granted, however unfair it might have been to Katharine. But the pope was at the time completely in the power of Katharine's nephew, the immensely powerful Emperor Charles V. It was bad luck for Henry; it was also bad luck for the Church of Rome for it led to England breaking away and forming a national church, the Church of England, controlled by the monarch. Henry married Anne, who gave him a daughter, Elizabeth, but no son. The marriage ended disastrously with Anne, convicted of adultery and treason, dying on the block in 1536 – the same year that Katharine, for many years a miserable prisoner, died almost alone.

At the time Henry broke with Rome the great tide of the Reformation was sweeping through Europe and had reached the shores of England, mainly due to the influence of men who would now be termed 'intellectuals', many of whom had sat at the feet of Luther at Wittenberg. The Reform movement in England was not, however, backed by a groundswell of popular support. Even the Lollards, who had represented a widespread discontent, had been persecuted out of existence for some decades. There were grumblings about the wealth and sloth of the monasteries, but envious greed had as much to do with this as morality.

Though Henry, who was something of a theologian, had listened to the Reformers, he had been a devoted son of the Church and had written a refutation of Luther for which Pope Leo x had given him the title of Defender of the Faith. His will to divorce Katharine and marry Anne may not have been the only reason for the break with Rome, but it was the prime one.

Suppose that Arthur had been that much physically stronger to survive and reign with Katharine, so strongly Catholic, at his side? The tide of Reformation in England might have been contained or swept back as it was in large parts of Europe. England might well have remained faithful to the Church of Rome, and the seeds of religious and political freedom which were germinating even under the despotic rule of the Tudors might never have flowered.

When Henry VIII died in 1547 he was in fact succeeded by his only legitimate son, Edward VI, the child of Jane Seymour. But Edward was only ten at the time, and died six years later, so that Henry's daughters, first Mary and later Elizabeth, came in turn to the throne.

Mary was Henry's daughter by his first wife, Katharine of Aragon. As Queen, Mary restored England's allegiance to the Church of Rome which had been broken by her father and married the Hapsburg Philip II of Spain, a paladin of the Church and heir to much of the world empire of his father, the Emperor Charles V.

If Mary and Philip had had a son or daughter to inherit the throne of England, the country might well have been reduced to a satellite of Spain with no outlet for its maritime energies except as agents of the Hapsburg Empire. Even if there had been a revolt in England, its chances of success would have been slim, for the Spaniards had great fleets and its infantry was at the time the most formidable military force in Europe.

But Mary died childless in 1558 and Elizabeth came to the throne and provided the leadership under which the English genius flowered in many fields with unsurpassed daring and imagination.

On the death of Queen Elizabeth I, King James VI of Scotland inherited the throne of England and came south to be crowned James I of England, the founder of the ill-fated House of Stuart. His parents were Henry Stuart, Earl of Darnley, and Mary, Queen of Scots, who was finally beheaded by Queen Elizabeth I for her Roman Catholic affiliations and endless conspiracies.

James I's eldest son, Prince Henry Frederick, came to London in 1603 with his mother, Anne of Denmark, in the footsteps of his father. He was nine years old and a strong and lively boy. When he was twelve the French Ambassador, de la Broderie, wrote of him: 'He is a particular lover of horses and what belongs to them, but is not fond of hunting and when he goes to it it is rather for the pleasure of galloping than that which the dogs give him.'

In June 1610, when Henry was sixteen, the King created him Prince of Wales and he formed his own court at St James's. It was a happy release for the young prince, for across the park at Whitehall his father's court was a squalid centre for drunkenness, crime and unnatural vice. James I was a pederast and lavished titles, lands and jewels on the young men whose cheeks he unashamedly kissed in public. The most notable of these were a Scottish page, Robert Carr, who became Earl of Rochester before being dismissed for his part in a notorious murder by poisoning, and the more formidable George Villiers, who was swiftly raised through the ranks of the peerage to become Duke of Buckingham.

The court of St James's soon became the resort of those who found the atmosphere at Whitehall distasteful. The Prince of Wales himself began to criticize his father, and word of this was duly carried to the King, who made the curious remark, 'Will he bury me alive?' This may have been a reference to the punishment meted out to homosexuals by the ancient German tribes.

By the time he was eighteen various projects of marriage had been suggested to the Prince of Wales but, although they might have strengthened the Stuart dynasty politically, he turned them down – a sign of independence rare at that time. He told his father and the ministers that he was thinking of travelling to Germany to find a bride for himself among the princesses there. He was studying military history and naval matters and beginning to take an interest in how the country was governed. Francis Bacon said of him that he was slow of speech, pertinent of question, patient in listening and of strong understanding. His manner was princely without condescension, courteous without familiarity.

Then suddenly this prince of so much promise was struck down by a fever in October 1612 and died within a few days. For a healthy young man to die so quickly gave rise to stories that he had been poisoned – but such rumours were common at the time, due partially to medical ignorance. Later it was proved, almost conclusively, that he died of typhoid fever.

So Prince Charles, the second son, became heir to the throne and succeeded his father in 1625 at the age of twenty-five as Charles I. He had been a weak and sickly child and though he grew up to be a handsome man of princely presence his character remained weak. To achieve his ambition of ruling without Parliament he relied on the strengths of others, Thomas Wentworth, Earl of Strafford, and Archbishop Laud, as well as his wife, Henrietta Maria of France, the granddaughter of Catherine de' Medici. Time and time again, when he had been defeated in the Civil War, powerful moderate elements in Parliament tried to arrange a compromise which would have left him on the throne. But he broke faith with a deviousness which only proved his weakness.

But, so far as one can tell, if Henry Frederick had lived to be king he would have been of a strong, independent mind, but willing to listen. He might have come to terms with a Parliament which had for a long time been asserting its rights to play a greater part in governing the nation. A compromise might have been reached in which the king retained considerable executive powers whilst acting within the framework of the consensus of opinion in Parliament. The monarch might have exercised the amplitude of powers granted to, say, the President of the United States of America, but for life, not for a term of years.

On the other hand, Henry Frederick might have decided that the struggle for power between monarch and Parliament could only be decided by force. If his early signs of ability and diligence had developed by the time he became king, perhaps he might have won the battle. Parliament and its supporters in the country might have been defeated and Henry Frederick might have successfully imposed absolute rule. Such a turn in events in British history now seems almost unthinkable, running counter to the slow, but deliberate development of Parliamentary rule. But who can tell?

Charles I was beheaded at Whitehall in 1649. At the Restoration his elder son became Charles II, and reigned in luxurious ease, keeping his Catholic faith to himself until his deathbed. He was succeeded by his younger brother, yet another second son, James II. But James, a man of some ability and marked diligence, threw his inheritance away by his bigoted folly.

The English aristocracy and the rising middle class had organized or applauded with enthusiasm the Restoration of the Stuarts after the death of Cromwell. But they had no wish to return to the personal rule of Charles I which had caused the Civil War. Wherever their loyalties had lain in that struggle, the men who had power in England were now determined that in future they themselves would rule the country through Parliament. England had welcomed a king back on the throne to free itself from the tyranny of Cromwell's rule by the Major-Generals, but had no intention of now suffering another form of tyranny – especially one linked to Roman Catholicism. James had two daughters by his first marriage to Anne Hyde – Mary, married to William of Orange, and Anne – both of whom had been brought up as Protestants. James, on the other hand, was a fervent Roman Catholic, and this, combined with his tyrannical rule, finally induced powerful factions in England to invite William of Orange to come over with an army from Holland and get rid of him. There followed the Glorious Revolution of 1688, which finally established the supremacy of Parliament and the Church of England. The settlement marked not only the defeat of James II, but also the final, posthumous defeat of his father, Charles I.

Mary then ruled jointly with her husband as William and Mary, and they were succeeded by her younger sister, Anne, who ruled from 1702 to 1714. So after James II the crown again passed to two daughters who, in normal circumstances, would not have come to the throne for James had had a son in 1688 by his second wife, Mary of Modena; but it was that year that he lost his throne and became an exile in France, with his wife and son, James Stuart, later to be called the Old Pretender.

It could not be said that Queen Anne had a happy life. By her husband Prince George of Denmark, she had seventeen miscarriages and a son who soon died. To preserve the Protestant succession the throne was to pass to the descendants of Charles I's sister, Elizabeth, who had married Frederick, the Elector Palatine, who was a Lutheran. Anne had at times a troubled conscience about her father, King James, who had died in exile in 1701, and there were widespread plots to restore his son, James Stuart, on her death. But Anne, though sometimes tempted, never gave real support to them and, when she died, the Elector George of Hanover, grandson of Elizabeth, came to England and was crowned George I without opposition.

In the early nineteenth century, William IV, who came to the throne in 1830, was in fact the third son of George III. As Prince William, Duke of Clarence, he had led a colourful career in the Royal Navy. His eldest brother succeeded to the throne as George IV, but died without heirs. The second son, Frederick, Duke of York, had also died without issue. So William became king, and reigned with a lot of common-sense until 1837 when, since he left no legitimate family, the throne passed to the daughter of his youngest brother the Duke of Kent – his niece, Victoria.

Victoria's reign lasted until 22 January 1901, and her eldest son, the Prince of Wales, succeeded her as Edward VII. But when he died in 1910, he was succeeded by his second son, George V, grandfather of Queen Elizabeth II.

7

The first son born to the Prince of Wales (later King Edward VII) was Prince Albert Victor, 'Eddy', later created Duke of Clarence. George was born a year later in 1865. Eddy grew up to be a congenitally lazy young man. It was almost a disease. He was quite incapable of concentrating on any mental activity whatsoever. Rather taller than his brother and sisters, he had large appealing eyes and brown wavy hair. His neck was so elongated that he had to wear very high collars which gave him a nickname of 'collars-and-cuffs'. This languid young man, however, developed a fierce sensuality to the astonishment and concern of his staff and equerries. He took his women not only from the upper classes, but from the streets.

Women found him attractive, apart from his exalted station in life. Princess Hélène, daughter of the Comte de Paris, grandson of King Louis Philippe and heir to the French throne, if the Bourbons were ever restored, was very much in love with him. Although she was a Roman Catholic, neither Queen Victoria nor the Prince of Wales were opposed to a match if she became a member of the Church of England. The Comte de Paris then decided that, if she would have to become a Protestant, the pope's consent must first be obtained. This was refused and that was the end of that romance. But Eddy was now twenty-six and Victoria wanted to see him married. She had in mind Princess May of Teck, a daughter of her first cousin, Princess Mary Adelaide of Cambridge. Victoria favoured May partly because her father, Prince Franz of Teck, had brought fresh vigorous blood into the family through his mother, a beautiful Hungarian. Victoria knew that there were signs of degeneration in the British royal family from in-breeding and was determined to do something about it. So Eddy and May became engaged and arrangements were being made for the wedding when, in January 1891, whilst he was at Sandringham, he caught influenza which turned to pneumonia and proved fatal. George was now the eldest son and after a decent interval he in turn became engaged to Princess May and in due course married her. Victoria wrote to him: 'Let me now say how thankful I am that this great and so long and ardently wished for event is settled and I gladly give my consent to what I pray may be for your happiness and for the country's good.' The old Queen could afford to be affectionate for she had got her way – a strong, healthy woman of her choice had been brought into the family to bear the children of the royal line.

With hindsight it was probably just as well for the British monarchy that George became king rather than Eddy, who might well have surrounded the court with sordid scandal and brought it into disrepute at a time when the great European dynasties were falling fast. By the end of the First World War the Romanovs had been eliminated in Russia by the 1917 Revolution; the Hapsburgs fell with the Austro-Hungarian Empire in 1918; the Hohenzollerns fled from Germany in the same year. The ensuing twenties were a time of unemployment,

Queen Mary with her two eldest sons, both of whom were to reign. One became Edward VIII who abdicated and became the Duke of Windsor, the other succeeded as George VI.

A painting of Prince George (right), who was to become King George V, with his elder brother Albert Victor, both wearing midshipman's uniform. Prince Albert Victor, the heir to the throne, died just before his marriage.

poverty and unrest and even in stable Britain a fear of revolution disturbed the peace of mind of the propertied classes.

King George, with his strait-laced, boring court and his quarter-deck sense of discipline and duty, was a symbol of stability in a world that seemed to have gone mad. He was limited in his outlook and his small circle of friends were mainly great landowners who shared his obsession for shooting game birds; but he showed at one decisive moment political sagacity of a high order. After a general election in January 1924, the Conservatives lost their overall majority. The largest party in the House of Commons was Labour, which had never held office. With Liberal support it could form a minority government. It is difficult now to appreciate the hysteria which this prospect caused among the middle and upper classes. It was to them as if the Bolshevik Revolution was to be repeated in Britain with all its horrors. George remained calm and sent for Mr Ramsay MacDonald, the Labour leader, to form a government. Throughout, the King behaved not just correctly, but with friendliness. When the cabinet had been formed he wrote to his mother, Queen Alexandra, of whom he was almost over-fond: 'I have been making the acquaintance of all the Ministers in turn and I must say they all seem to be very intelligent and they take things very seriously. They have different ideas to ours as they are all socialists, but they ought to be given a chance and ought to be treated fairly.'

If George had behaved arrogantly or patronizingly, the Labour Party could well have become anti-monarchical. But that first step in 1924 led to harmonious relationships that have made successive Labour governments staunch monarchists and helped to bring new strength to the kings and queens who have followed. If George reacted to the situation instinctively, his instincts were profoundly right.

George v was followed to the throne by his eldest son, David, who ruled as Edward viii – but only for one year. Queen Elizabeth must remember the year of 1936 all too vividly, for her whole life was changed when her father, a second son, came to the throne as George vi on the unforeseeable abdication of his brother, Edward. Overnight she became heir to the throne.

Her father had been totally unprepared. There is poignancy in his remark to Louis Mountbatten as they watched Edward go out into the night after he had abdicated: 'Dickie, this is absolutely terrible. I never wanted this to happen; I'm quite unprepared for it. David [the family name for Edward] has been trained for this all his life. I've never even seen a State Paper. I'm only a naval officer, it's the only thing I know about.' He was at that time just approaching his forty-first birthday.

It was not only his lack of training that handicapped him. He had never been strong and was forced by ill-health to give up an active naval career during the First World War. He also suffered from a severe impediment of speech which by valiant struggles over many years he managed to master. Perhaps in compensation, however, the gods were kind to him in his choice of Elizabeth Bowes-Lyon as his wife. Her love, her infectious enjoyment of life and strength of character enriched him; their two daughters, Elizabeth and Margaret, brought happiness and fun. With such a family background he was able to rise to the challenge.

It was a very hard challenge, for his elder brother had enjoyed for many years a phenomenal popularity. He had laid the foundations of it when, as a young man, he had spent much time on the western front during the First World War. Although against his will he was kept out of the front line, he was very much around and about. The men who survived the slaughter felt he had known and cared about them and when they came back to endure the poverty of the twenties and the thirties he still had their loyalty, despite spending much of his life as a playboy. He retained even in his middle years a boyish charm and the young set of the establishment knew he was in revolt against the stuffy traditions of the past.

The press had sedulously built him up as an adventurous, unconventional Prince Charming who was creating a new royal style more suited to the times. He refused to marry any of the eligible princesses suggested to him, but was content to have a steady mistress, Mrs Freda Dudley Ward, for fifteen years. Then in 1934 he abruptly and with a certain lack of feeling broke off the relationship and not long after met the woman who was to change his life, Wallis Simpson. After he became king on 20 January 1936 it was increasingly clear to Stanley Baldwin, the Prime Minister of a national but predominantly Conservative Government, that he intended to wed her. The Government decided that Edward VIII would not be permitted to remain on the throne, if he was so resolved. Though the crisis became critical the British public remained ignorant of the situation; both Edward and Baldwin managed to prevent the press proprietors from printing anything about it. The final chapter of the story was breathtakingly brief. It lasted just over a week. The storm broke on 3 December when the press finally decided to publish the story – probably at Mr Baldwin's instigation. Edward, for so long accustomed to public adulation, was unnerved by the criticism. 'They don't want me,' he said with despair after reading a leading article in the *Birmingham Post*. He finally accepted he would have to abdicate to marry Wallis Simpson and on 10 December signed his throne away. The next day he made a farewell broadcast to the nation, said goodbye to his family and embarked on a destroyer for France. It was all over in eight days.

Mr Baldwin had handled the matter most adroitly to ensure the least possible disturbance to the nation. For some time there were mutterings among the working class that the King had been got rid of because he had wanted to do something about the terrible unemployment. In November 1936, during what proved to be his last official tour, Edward had been to south Wales and seen some of the worst of the depression. 'Something must be done to find them work,' he had said, and those words were the basis of the myth of the king who cared.

The establishment and the press, however, rallied round the new King. He needed encouragement; he was bewildered. In addition, Edward had behaved badly to him during the crisis, telling him nothing and cancelling appointments to see him at the last minute, although he knew very well that his brother would have to pick up the pieces when he abdicated.

Speaking in the slow, measured tones he had to adopt to overcome his stammer, King George said to his Privy Councillors when he first met them: 'I meet you today in circumstances which are without parallel in the history of our country . . . with my wife and helpmeet by my side, I take up the heavy task which lies before me. In it I look for the support of all my peoples.' As Queen, Elizabeth certainly proved an admirable 'helpmeet' to her husband and became one of the most popular consorts in British history – a popularity which has lasted during her many years as Queen Mother since the death of George VI in 1952.

During the Second World War the new King and Queen forged strong new links between the monarchy and the nation. During the disastrous years of 1940 and 1941 before the tide of war had turned, they stayed in or near London and their visits to blitzed areas there and elsewhere gave great confidence to the public. 'We suddenly felt that if the King was there, everything was all right and the rest of England was behind us,' said one of the survivors of a heavy air raid on Coventry. Though in failing health, the King lived to see Britain victorious and shared a few of the years when the country was facing the future with hope. He was not a very clever man; he did not possess the gifts which easily bring popularity; but he won his way through by grit, a sense of duty and a deep love of his country.

As for the elder brother whom George had succeeded as king, he showed a lamentable side of his nature when France fell in 1940. He was then the Duke of Windsor and living in Paris with Wallis as his Duchess. When the Germans approached Paris the Windsors went to their house in the South of France and from there to neutral Portugal, with as much as possible of the Duchess's extensive wardrobe and fabulous jewellery packed into a luggage trailer attached to their car. In Portugal there is little doubt that German agents were in touch with the Duke during 1940 when the fall of Britain seemed likely. If Britain had been in imminent danger of being occupied by the Germans there is little doubt that the royal family would have been evacuated to Canada, as symbols of the determination to carry on the struggle from overseas. It is not too fanciful to imagine the Germans in such circumstances facilitating the return of the Duke and Duchess to Britain to reign as puppet king and queen. If this had happened, what would have been the future of the monarchy when finally the Americans and the troops of Britain and the Empire abroad had liberated the country? It might have proved impossible for George and Elizabeth, after years in exile in Canada, to re-establish themselves in a land which had endured not only occupation, but another king and queen who had been creatures of the Germans. It might have spelled the end of the British monarchy.

Meanwhile, as the Queen and Prince Philip planned the education and career of their second son, it is likely that they remembered the experience of her own father who came so suddenly and with so little preparation to the throne.

It is an almost irresistible temptation to find a pattern in history, and this account of second sons and daughters who have reigned in England during the last five hundred years inevitably stirs the imagination. The search for some design is at its best no more than a pastime for an idle hour.

Until the Declaration of Rights in 1689 denied the rule of executive decree, the sovereign exercised great power, at times so absolute that his or her decisions affected the fate of the whole nation. Since then the supremacy of Parliament has left the sovereign with little direct power, but a measure of influence largely determined by the personality of the individual reigning.

It would be fair to say that Queen Elizabeth II has by her efforts strengthened the crown as a unifying force in the nation and Commonwealth. With ever-present threats of tyranny the monarchy has in her reign emerged as an ultimate rallying point for our freedom.

It is, therefore, important who succeeds her, and what sort of person he is likely to prove. It is unlikely that Prince Andrew will ever succeed to the throne, but as the second son he can play a significant role. This book is an attempt to find out what sort of young man he is and describe the influences that have shaped him.

2

Joining the Family

Queen Elizabeth II was safely delivered of her third child and second son, who was to be named Andrew, at 3.30 p.m. on Friday, 19 February 1960 and for those with a taste for astrology Mars was in conjunction with Venus.

Andrew became on his birth second in line to succession to the throne after his brother Charles, Prince of Wales, and his sister Anne was relegated to third place. By his birth he was a prince of the royal House of Windsor, entitled to be called as long as he lived 'Your Royal Highness', and a member of the most prestigious royal family in the world. It was also a very rich family and the newly-born prince would, failing unforeseeable disasters, always be financially secure apart from the grants made by the state to the members of the royal family. In the lottery of life, he had been born fortunate.

The birth had gone so smoothly that within a few hours the Queen was sitting up in bed, looking extremely well, and going through one of the official 'boxes' of government documents that had followed her around ever since she came to the throne eight years earlier on 6 February 1952. She was said to be delighted to have added to her family at the age of thirty-four after an interval of nearly ten years since Princess Anne was born on 15 August 1950. The first-born, Charles, had arrived two years earlier on 14 November 1948.

Her delight was shared by her husband, Prince Philip, then thirty-nine, who was by her side at Buckingham Palace, and by her family, especially her mother, Queen Elizabeth, the Queen Mother. When the news was announced the whole nation took pleasure in the event – and there was a certain feeling of relief mingled with the pleasure, for Elizabeth in her years on the throne had evoked affection to add to the traditional loyalty to the monarchy. There was pleasure too in the worldwide Commonwealth to which the Queen had paid many visits and in many other countries where she had won respect both as a queen and as a person. Messages of congratulation poured into the Palace Post Office. Flags were flown, salutes fired and the House of Commons sent its customary loyal message.

The British were going through a reasonably prosperous period. Memories of

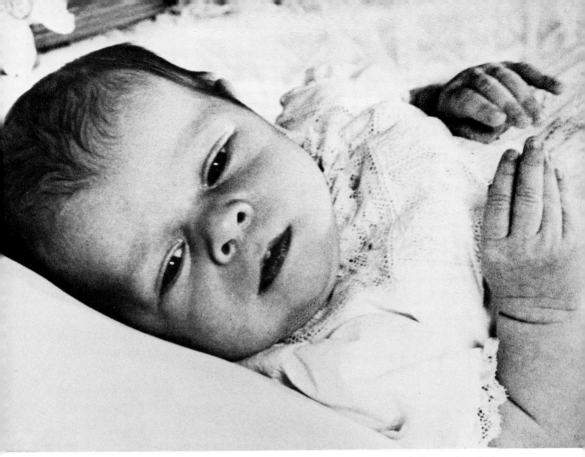

Above In the Music Room at Buckingham Palace the new Prince was christened and given the names Andrew Albert Christian Edward.

Above At the Tower of London the Honourable Artillery Company salutes the birth on 19 February 1960 of Queen Elizabeth's second son in traditional style.

the restrictions of the war and immediate postwar period were fading into the past. The Conservative Party was in power with Mr Macmillan – Supermac to the cartoonists – as Prime Minister, and his slogan, 'You've never had it so good', had some relevance for living standards were rising, unemployment was low, money easy to raise and prices fairly stable. It seemed, in a way, symbolic that at such a time the Queen should increase her family. It was, by and large, a happy time.

The Queen and Philip had wanted to add to their family for some years. Personally, they liked children; in addition, for dynastic reasons an addition or two would strengthen the monarchy. The Queen's decision to wait for so long had made most people think that she did not want any more children after Charles and Anne, but, in fact, circumstances had not in the intervening years been favourable.

Princess Elizabeth, as she then was, had married Prince Philip on 20 November 1947, when she was twenty-one. She was twenty-two when she gave birth to Charles and twenty-four when she had Anne. By that time, however, her father, King George VI, never a strong man, was already failing in health. Elizabeth, as heir to the throne, was soon made conscious that she would probably succeed to the throne much earlier than had seemed likely even a few years previously. Her love for her father made her anxious and sad; she was still a shy person and worried at the thought of the responsibilities she might have to assume any day. It was not a time when she could afford to be incapacitated by child-bearing.

The King had hoped to make a long Commonwealth tour at the beginning of 1952, but his health made it impossible and Elizabeth, accompanied by Philip, went in his stead. He went to see them off at London Airport and looked a very sick man. It was the last time Elizabeth was to see her father alive, for it was only a few days later, when she was in East Africa, that the news of his death was broken to her.

Elizabeth, now queen two months before her twenty-sixth birthday, faced challenges that must at times have seemed insurmountable to her. This was the time when Prince Philip was of immense help. He was ebullient, confident and loving, and smoothed out the problems which were more psychological than real. With a devoted staff around her the Queen learned the routine of her position as a constitutional monarch. At the same time she was involved in the intricate planning for her Coronation in June 1953. This was followed by a splendid world tour of the Commonwealth which broadened her horizons. There were state visits to friends and allies, France, Italy, Denmark, Sweden, Norway and Portugal. These were years when the Queen had to give herself entirely to her tasks. They were splendidly memorable years for she was young and strong, but there was no time to think of increasing her family.

There were, too, in the fifties family problems. Her sister, Princess Margaret, fell in love with a handsome equerry, Group-Captain Peter Townsend, whose marriage had ended in divorce. Margaret was a beautiful, lively young woman, artistic and musical, who had inherited some of the Stuart mercurial charm. But, different as she was from her sister, the Queen had shared her early life and felt for her during the months of emotional turmoil and worldwide publicity culminating in a renunciation which now, with hindsight, was probably tragic.

While Prince Philip was away on a long cruise on his own in the royal yacht, *Britannia*, the Queen had to face alone the appalling consequences of the Suez crisis in November 1956, which caused rifts in the Commonwealth and a coolness in the overwhelmingly powerful ally, the United States. When Philip returned it was clear that absence, as so often when there is real love, had strengthened the relationship. But it had been a wearing time for the Queen.

As the fifties drew to a close, however, the Queen entered a more tranquil period. She had not only learned how to do her job, she had learned to do it superbly well. The monarchy was, if anything, more popular than ever. Her health was good and she felt she could cope with the months of pregnancy without any great disturbance to her duties.

When Andrew was born he was the first child to be born to a reigning monarch since Princess Beatrice, the last of Queen Victoria's nine children, in 1857. The christening took place in the music room at Buckingham Palace, and he was given the names of Andrew Albert Christian Edward. Andrew was the name of Prince Philip's father; Albert had been the first name of the Queen's father although he reigned as King George VI and it recalled the name of Queen Victoria's consort who had given the dynasty its title of the House of Saxe-Coburg-Gotha, subsequently changed to the House of Windsor; Christian was a name favoured by the Danish royal family which had provided in the nineteenth century a King of Greece from whom Prince Philip is descended; Edward is a traditional name in the British royal family and could be regarded as a family gesture to the ageing Duke of Windsor.

Andrew's life in the nursery was presided over by Mrs Mabel Anderson, a Scottish children's nurse who had got her job through an advertisement in a nurses' magazine. She was extremely capable, combining firmness and expertise with the right measure of affection for her charge. There was not just the nursery at Buckingham Palace; there were others at Windsor Castle, Balmoral and Sandringham.

At week-ends and during holidays the Queen made sure that she saw a good deal of her new son. But even at Buckingham Palace in the midst of her duties she found time to be with him, especially on 'Mabel's night out' when she gave him his bath, changed him and put him to bed. In a way Andrew had brought back to the Queen and Prince Philip a renewed sense of youth and fun.

After a few months Andrew was brought down to his parents most mornings after breakfast to have a look round with the bright blue eyes he had inherited from his father. He had his outings in the pram, at first in the spacious grounds of Buckingham Palace, later in St James's Park when a plain-clothes detective would accompany the nurse. At the week-ends he would travel in one of the royal cars to Windsor. In the autumn he would go with his parents, brother and sister to Balmoral in the royal train for the ritual two months in the Highlands where family life was almost undisturbed by ceremony and crowds. After Christmas there was the month at Sandringham in Norfolk where the peace of life was broken only by the guns of the shooting parties.

As these early years passed Andrew became conscious of the family he had joined. Apart from his mother, the most important person was his father, Prince Philip, Duke of Edinburgh. It is as well to stress this for, because of the exalted position of the Queen, there is a tendency to forget that Prince Philip, as husband and father, is head of the family and, leaving aside the Queen's position as sovereign, is conscious of the fact. In private life he is the man, Elizabeth the wife and the children are his offspring. He is a man of strong character who accepts his responsibilities and would never allow his rights to be infringed. It is he who has been the dominant influence in the upbringing and education of the children. The Queen has always deferred to his judgment – even though there have been disagreements.

Compared with the sheltered, secure life of the British royal family, Prince Philip's was until his marriage adventurous and even uncertain. His father was Prince Andrew of Greece, son of the King of Greece who had married a niece of the Tsar Alexander II. His mother was Princess Alice of Battenberg, daughter of Prince Louis of Battenberg who had married a cousin, Princess Victoria of Hesse.

Princess Alice had four daughters and then seven years later, on 10 June 1921, gave birth to a son, Prince Philip. He was born in troubled times, for the Greeks suffered overwhelming disasters in a war with Turkey and Prince Andrew commanded one of the defeated Greek army corps. The Greeks with Balkan fury looked for scapegoats, turned on the royal family and arrested Prince Andrew. In the frenzy of the times it was very likely he would be shot to assuage national pride. He was saved by a British agent acting on behalf of the Government. King George v exerted all his influence behind the scenes. He was conscious that he had been reluctant to give refuge to the Russian royal family in Britain and their subsequent murder by the Bolsheviks lay on his conscience. All Prince Andrew's family were

Prince Charles, eleven years old, has a look at his new brother, Andrew.

Above A big smile from Prince Andrew as he sits on the lap of his grandmother, Queen Elizabeth, the Queen Mother, on her six-tieth birthday.

Below Happy Andrew gives a hand to his father, Prince Philip, and to his sister, Princess Anne, who was nearly ten.

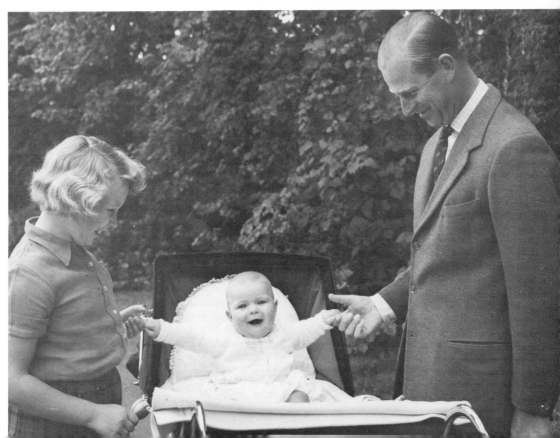

saved and the infant Philip and his four elder sisters were picked up by a British warship from the island of Corfu where the Greek royal family had a beautiful summer palace.

Many great monarchies had fallen at the end of the First World War and western Europe was a shelter for royal and noble exiles, sometimes penniless, all conscious of lost privileges and grandeur. Philip's family did not fare too badly. All four sisters married very grand German princes who had retained large estates in the new republican Germany. Prince Andrew retired to the south of France on a reasonable retainer from the family, enjoyed himself and took no further interest in wife, daughters or son.

Fortunately for young Philip his mother's family was rich and powerful in England. They had sympathy for Princess Alice. Completely deaf, married to an uncaring husband, she found consolation in religion. As the years passed she removed herself from the world, eventually finding a quiet life within the Greek Orthodox Church in a small community of religious women.

For a Battenberg it was out of character, for the family has achieved wealth and position through a combination of good looks, charm, ability and determination. The Battenbergs had a romantic origin in the middle of the nineteenth century. Prince Alexander of Hesse went to St Petersburg where his sister, Marie, had married the heir to the Russian throne (the future Alexander II who was assassinated by revolutionaries in 1881). Prince Alexander, handsome and amusing, was a favourite at court, given a commission in the Russian army and the then Tsar, Nicholas I, wanted him to marry his niece, the Grand Duchess Catherine. Everything seemed set for a brilliant career until Alexander fell in love with the Countess Julie von Hauke, a rather lowly lady-in-waiting of mixed Polish and German blood. He eloped with her. The Tsar was furious with him, so was his brother, Louis, the Grand Duke of Hesse. The marriage between Alexander and Julie was morganatic because she was not of sufficiently noble blood. But Alexander's brother relented enough to create her Princess of Battenberg, a small district in Hesse, with a castle, Heiligenberg, at Darmstadt. The five children were all to be given the rank of Prince or Princess.

The eldest was Louis, the youngest Henry and both came to England where they had a great success with Queen Victoria. Henry married her daughter, Princess Beatrice. Louis married her granddaughter, Princess Victoria of Hesse, and made a brilliant career in the Royal Navy. He was First Sea Lord when war broke out in 1914, but was forced to resign soon after because of a venomous press campaign against his German background. Later in the war feeling against the Germans rose so high that King George V changed the name of his dynasty from Saxe-Coburg-Gotha to Windsor. The Battenbergs became Mountbattens and Louis was created Marquis of Milford Haven.

Louis had four children – George became the second Marquis, Louise married King Gustav of Sweden, Alice married Prince Andrew and the youngest, another Louis, was the prestigious Earl Mountbatten of Burma.

So Prince Philip, the son of Alice and Andrew, has the blood of many great families in his veins – and also that of his great-grandmother, Julie von Hauke, for love of whom Prince Alexander threw up a brilliant career and the hand of a Romanov. All these strains are in the children of the Queen and Prince Philip – Charles, Anne, Andrew and Edward (born in 1964).

It was this family of Battenbergs, now Mountbattens, who were able to look after the young exiled Prince Philip. His grandmother, Victoria, by then the Dowager Marchioness of Milford Haven, was the first to help. Later his uncle, then Lord Louis Mountbatten, played a considerable role.

Philip was sent first to an expensive preparatory school at St Cloud outside Paris where many of the pupils came from expatriate English and American families. Then he came to England and was sent to Cheam, a preparatory school which had traditional links with the Navy. But his sister, Theodora, had close relations through her husband, Prince Berthold of Baden, with a school at Salem in South Germany which had been founded by Kurt Hahn, an educationalist of originality. Philip was sent there, but Hahn, a Jew, had to go into exile when Hitler came to power. He founded a new school at Gordonstoun in Scotland and Philip was one of the handful of pupils who followed him there. He was proving an outstanding boy, intelligent and industrious and a good all-rounder.

With a grandfather who had been First Sea Lord and an uncle, Lord Louis, who was making a name for himself in the Navy, there was a certain inevitability about the next step in Philip's career. He went to Dartmouth to train as a British naval officer although the Greek royal family had had hopes he might join the Greek navy. George VI, who had been to Dartmouth himself, went with the Queen and Elizabeth and Margaret to inspect the college a few months before the outbreak of war. It was the first time that Princess Elizabeth, then thirteen, met the handsome naval cadet of eighteen, Philip, who was to be her husband.

It was by this time very unlikely that King George and Queen Elizabeth would have another child. If a son had been born he would have taken precedence over Elizabeth, but this was not to happen, so she grew up in the knowledge that, subject to the vicissitudes of life, she would one day be queen. The choice of a husband became important not only to her and her family; it was of national significance.

If Prince Philip had not existed, it would have been necessary to invent him. Prince Philip was indeed supremely eligible. He had been born a royal prince. On his father's side he was connected with the British royal family, for Queen Alexandra, the wife of Edward VII, was the sister of King George I of Greece, who was his grandfather. On his mother's side, her mother had been a granddaughter of Queen Victoria. He was of good physique, five years older than Elizabeth and during the war served with distinction in the Navy. With powerful relatives he had no need to worry that for the time being he had no money of his own.

As it happened everything fell into place. When Philip was home on leave he visited Elizabeth and as the friendship deepened they wrote to each other. Elizabeth was deeply in love and Philip was as eager a suitor as any young woman could desire. The marriage on 20 November 1947 in Westminster Abbey was immensely popular and brought more than a touch of colour to a country still enduring austerity in the immediate postwar years.

Before the marriage Prince Philip renounced his foreign titles and became a British subject. There was the question of the family name he should adopt. On his father's side the Greek royal family descended from the Danish royal house of Schleswig-Holstein-Sonderburg-Glücksburg, but it was decided that Philip should take the name of his mother's family, Mountbatten. It was the ultimate triumph for a family that had sprung into being only a century before as Battenbergs, the children of a morganatic marriage.

Years later, in 1960, the Queen gave formal notice of the change of surname of the family. 'While I and my children shall continue to be styled and known as the House and family of Windsor, my descendants shall bear the name of Mountbatten-Windsor.' When Princess Anne married she was described on the marriage certificate as Anne Elizabeth Alice Louise Mountbatten-Windsor.

When Elizabeth came to the throne in 1952 Prince Philip hoped to be able to emulate Prince Albert, the brilliant consort of Queen Victoria, who, in his short life, had played a significant role in the life of the nation. In this he was bound to be frustrated. The direct power of the crown had in the intervening century been much eroded by the development of democracy and Elizabeth, though deeply in love, was not, like Queen Victoria, a woman who would consider devolving her numerous royal duties.

Philip will be remembered by the phrase 'pull your finger out' which he used in the early years of the reign. It summed up his frequent exhortations to the nation. He was urging more and better production from management and workers alike. It was a message that no doubt needed to be proclaimed, but the British did not like it coming from the husband of the Queen. The members of the royal family are given loyalty, reverence and the money to provide splendour as they perform the rituals of constitutional monarchy. They are symbols of the unity of the nation, above the hurly-burly of life. The British feel instinctively that, if the royal family starts to express opinions about the business of life, it is endangering its real function. Gradually, not easily, Prince Philip learned the lesson and found new fields of endeavour which won him sincere praise and respect. The creation of the

Duke of Edinburgh's Award Scheme in Britain and the Commonwealth showed his organizational abilities and has proved an inspiration for youth of lasting value. His spirit of adventure and his mánliness have been of immense significance, not only here but in the world beyond at a time when Britain was shedding an empire and being accused of decadence.

Philip has charm and grace, but he is not an easy man. He is a perfectionist and does not suffer fools gladly – and he has to meet many in his position. His manner has never lost something of the quarterdeck and with it a touch of arrogance from his father's family. He is by nature authoritarian and does not appreciate that often democracy has to make do with compromises that are more than a little shoddy. He likes 'a good press', but does not appear to have appreciated that you must learn to take the rough with the smooth when you are in the public eye – and, by and large, the British press is very loyal.

It cannot be said that he has made many close friends, but that may be because he feels that in his position he cannot afford friendship. But it has meant that, as the years have passed, he has stood alone. He has, however, drawn great strength from his family. He has kept in touch with his sisters and their families in Germany, finding satisfaction in a kinship that he lacks in England outside his immediate family.

But, above all, he has been a caring father to his children. He has watched over their upbringing, tried to cure their failings, encouraged them when they encountered difficulties, worked hard to retain their confidence. If he is tough with them, it is because he knows their position and privileges could easily lead to self-indulgent weakness. Partly this is because he grew up in a broken family and knew what it was to have no father at hand. Partly it is because he is a man who takes all his responsibilities seriously. But, in addition, he has been quite determined on his rights as a father.

When Andrew was in the nursery he was often visited by his sister, Anne, who was not yet away at school. His brother, Prince Charles, saw him from time to time during his school holidays. There was, however, a gulf of years between Andrew and them which was in the early years unbridgeable, as would have been the case in any other family. Charles was eleven years and three months old and Anne nine and a half.

At the time Charles was having a rather unhappy time at his father's old preparatory school, Cheam, following two terms as a day boy at Hill House in Knightsbridge which had been interrupted by trouble with his tonsils. Charles just did not like being away at school and had retreated into himself. He complained bitterly to his parents, but Prince Philip convinced the Queen that he would just have to sweat it out and learn to cope. If he was taken away from school and his education entrusted to private tutors, there was every probability he would grow up an introverted person incapable of taking on the very important public role to which he had been born.

Charles was a shy and sensitive boy. Many other boys suffer from the same qualities when they are young, but in the case of Charles the situation was worse because as soon as he went out into the world he was conscious that everyone, boys and teachers alike, regarded him in a special light because he was Prince Charles, son of the Queen and heir to the throne. However hard everyone tried to treat him as just another boy, the barrier was there – and his sensitivity made it worse.

To add to the inevitable curiosity of boys and teachers, there was the pervasive influence of the media. Ever since his birth the appetite of the press, national and international, for news about him had been insatiable. Anecdotes, even the slightest, commanded high prices; so did photographs of him, especially if they had been taken in an unguarded moment. His detective was constantly on the alert and the atmosphere of anxious watchfulness affected the boy. At Cheam the grounds had to be extensively and expensively patrolled to guard against the intrusion of photographers and the strain told not only on Charles, but on teachers and boys, so that there were those who wished that the heir to the throne had been sent elsewhere to school.

With the admonitions of his father in his mind Charles did make an effort, but circumstances made it very hard for him. On 26 July 1958, when he was not yet ten, he was invited into the headmaster's study with a small party of other boys to look at a special television programme. The Queen announced that she was that day creating Charles Prince of Wales. The boys clapped and congratulated him, but Charles would have liked to sink through the floor. How could he and everyone else keep up the pretence that he was just another boy like everyone else at Cheam!

When Andrew was born his sister Anne was a plump, lively tomboy. She was fretting at home, for her parents had decided she would not go away to school until she was thirteen. She took classes at home under a governess with a small group of other girls, but she felt hemmed in. Her brother Charles hated being away at school, whilst she could not wait for the day. She was intelligent, rather wilful, got on well with other girls and could be very kind when her sympathies were aroused.

Horses were already her great interest. Like all the children of the royal family she was put on a pony almost before she could walk and took to it as a duck does to water. She and Charles shared two ponies, William and Greensleeves, when they were quite young. Like their mother they went to the famous riding school of the Smiths at Holyport near Windsor. Anne was an enthusiastic pupil who was sorry when the lesson was over. Soon after Andrew was born, Sir John Miller, the Crown Equerry, arranged for the purchase of a cream-coloured pony, Bandit, for

Andrew's first visit to the royal home at Balmoral in Scotland.

The first public appearance. On the balcony of Buckingham Palace the Queen holds up Andrew for inspection after she had attended the Trooping the Colour on Horse Guards Parade to celebrate her official birthday on 10 June 1961.

Charles and Anne, but it was Anne who took every opportunity to ride him. Sir John saw her interest and had a small cross-country course set up in the Home Park at Windsor. She was beginning her career as a horsewoman which would not only bring her fame but the friendship of a brilliant Olympic horseman, Mark Phillips, whom she was eventually to marry.

Apart from his parents and brother and sister there was his grandmother to complete Andrew's immediate family. The Queen Mother was sixty when Andrew was born and had been a widow for eight years; she had receded into the background with the grace that had come naturally to her all her life. Now she lived in Clarence House near the Palace and found great pleasure in lavishing affection on her grandchildren. When the Queen and Prince Philip were away on their frequent foreign trips, the Queen Mother gave the three children extra attention. They all loved her dearly, partly because of herself, partly – it must be admitted – because she tended to spoil them a little.

This then was Prince Andrew's family, the first family in Britain and the Commonwealth that was replacing the old Empire. Unlike the other great world powers, the head of state in Britain was the monarch who had been placed there by family succession, not by votes. There were other monarchies but none so prestigious or important as the British. It could be said fairly that Prince Andrew belonged to a family that by the attention and interest it evoked had no parallel in the world.

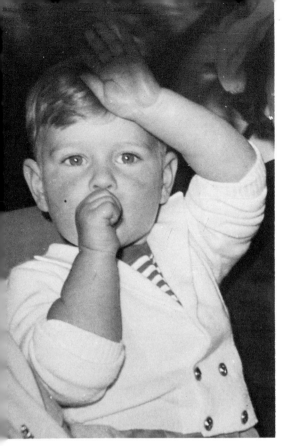

A comforting suck at the thumb as Andrew returns to London from Sandringham, the royal home in Norfolk.

Andrew showing an early interest in the land.

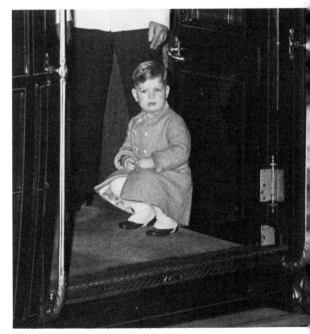

Andrew looks to the harness of one of the royal ponies while his mother looks on approvingly. The royal children are put on a pony almost before they can walk.

Andrew waits for the rest of the family to join the royal train at King's Cross. It was time for the New Year holiday at Sandringham.

3

A Merry Andrew

When Andrew was around one year old he was the subject of disagreeable enquiries by a Paris newspaper. It had been led to believe by a contact in London that there was something radically wrong with the young prince. It was said that there had been few photographs of Andrew because he was malformed. Journalists were sent here from Paris and rumours spread. The stories caused pain to the Queen and provoked anger in Prince Philip, but it was decided that the wisest policy was to make no comment. Later photographs of the young prince were circulated which showed him as a healthy, plump baby with no apparent defect.

As he became conscious of the world around him, he naturally took for granted the quite exceptional circumstances of his life. The furnishings of his nursery were ordinary enough, so were his nanny and her aides, but from time to time there were incursions which were real enough to him, but which would have seemed like a fairy-tale to most other children. His mother would come to see him sometimes of an evening wearing a magnificent ball-dress, her head crowned with a tiara glittering with jewels. His father might appear in a splendid uniform, covered with gold and shining stars. He was taken to the window of Buckingham Palace to see his mother, in uniform, on horseback riding away up the Mall surrounded by men in scarlet wearing great black bearskins for what he was told was her birthday parade. Or he might see her on a cold November day driving away in a golden coach escorted by soldiers on splendid horses and wearing great helmets with streaming plumes and be told his mother was going to open Parliament. These events, so extraordinary for most people, he naturally learned to take for granted.

When he went to play in the garden at Buckingham Palace there were great lawns stretching for acres, flower-beds blooming in meticulous order in perspectives that seemed endless. There was a lake; there were trees in abundance. It was larger than many public parks, but here there was no public.

When he travelled it was not by bus or tube or in an ordinary saloon car. He climbed into one of the great royal limousines, carpeted and spacious and in the

With an independent air Andrew strolls outside
Frogmore House on the Windsor estate.

Above left Andrew, now four, goes with the Queen to
see his new brother, Prince Edward, born on 10
March 1964.

Left At Smith's Lawn, Windsor, Andrew hurries to
watch the polo. Both his father and brother, Prince
Charles, are good players.

front was a uniformed driver and another smartly-dressed man whom in time he realized was always with him, his detective.

When he went by train he went into the nursery coach of the royal train, air-conditioned and sound-proof, with his own bedroom and a sitting-room and bathroom beyond. And when he went along the corridor to see his mother and father they would be sitting, not in an ordinary railway-coach, but in a luxurious sitting-room.

When he went by sea he travelled in the 413-foot-long royal yacht *Britannia*, magnificently appointed with a hand-picked crew who respond to orders given by a gesture, not by word of mouth. Andrew and his nurse had their own quarters, but he enjoyed walking the immaculate decks and being shown the bridge and engine-room by helpful officers.

And when later he went by air he travelled in one of the aircraft of the Queen's Flight and could walk around the cabin which was arranged as a comfortable lounge with armchairs, tables for newspapers and magazines and equipped with small kitchen and bar.

All this too Andrew grew up to take for granted.

When Andrew was four years old the Queen presented him with a young brother. He was born on 10 March 1964 and was christened Edward Antony Richard Louis. The Queen was thirty-eight and she was advised to take life easily for a few weeks. But she is a strong woman and was soon back on form.

Prince Charles had gone to Gordonstoun in May 1962, following in his father's footsteps. Princess Anne had been delighted to go away to boarding-school in the autumn of 1963. She was sent to Benenden, an expensive school in Kent with an excellent reputation. Charles had still not found his feet and found Gordonstoun even worse than Cheam, but he realized now that there was no alternative and settled down as best he could. Anne had no problems at Benenden and soon made friends, though at first she found the noise overwhelming, which was natural enough for a girl who had so far been educated at home with only one or two other girls to keep her company. But she was intelligent, worked hard enough to keep out of trouble, enjoyed the games – and found to her delight that there were riding lessons at a nearby stables.

Andrew was enjoying life, but at times life was not so pleasant for the staff. He was full of life and mischief, obstinate if he didn't get his own way, but capable of great charm when he felt like it. It was always easy to tell when he was around. There were shouts, laughter, angry cries and a determined curiosity to know what was going on. Mabel Anderson had her hands full teaching him rudimentary manners. At table there were many long tests of will before Andrew could be induced not to scoff his food as fast as he could and get back to his games.

He loved being with his father who in turn liked being with him. There was

Andrew wearing the Royal Stuart kilt at the Braemar Games which are held in September and regularly attended by the royal family on holiday at nearby Balmoral. Princess Anne by his side has her brother well under control.

nothing introspective about Andrew. There was no shyness such as had plagued his elder brother. Prince Philip taught him to swim in the indoor pool at Buckingham Palace and played with him in the gardens. When Prince Philip's relatives came over to stay they all said that he was just like his father had been at the same age – sometimes a nuisance, but full of life and very attractive.

But these halcyon days of almost complete freedom for Andrew were drawing to a close. When he was five the classroom, empty for years, was reopened and Miss Katherine Peebles, who had been governess to Charles and Anne, started to give him lessons. She was a wise, experienced woman who stood no nonsense with Andrew's rebelliousness and with skill funnelled his zest for life into useful channels. She was soon able to report that the boy showed signs of developing into a bright pupil once he had got used to the discipline. A few other boys of around the same age joined him later on. They came mainly from the families of court officials, but his cousin Viscount Linley was also sent to start on his three Rs. He was the son of Princess Margaret, who shortly after Andrew's birth had married Anthony Armstrong-Jones, a photographer of note, who was created Earl of Snowdon the following year with a second title of Viscount Linley which was, as is normal, given to the eldest son as a courtesy title.

It could not be said that all Prince Andrew's fellow-pupils enjoyed his company at all times. He had a streak of aggressiveness and could throw his weight around when he was in the mood. There was, however, a girl in the class who stood up to him and gave as good as she got. Her name was Katie Seymour, and she was the same age as Andrew. She was the daughter of Major Raymond Seymour, a director of Whitbread's the brewers, who was an extra equerry to the Queen Mother. They made friends and from the age of nine Andrew spent a few days of the summer holidays for several years with the Seymours at their house at Bembridge, Isle of Wight, a fashionable yachting harbour near Cowes. Prince Philip, a fine yachtsman and patron of the sport, was nearly always at the Cowes Regatta using the royal yacht as his headquarters at the same time as Andrew was staying at Bembridge. Katie was invited on board the *Britannia* which did no harm to his prestige with her. Philip taught Andrew to sail and the August days were filled with fun and laughter, except when his father saw a photographers' launch bearing down on them and the language became stronger than the wind.

Andrew's parents decided not to repeat the experiment they had made with Charles and send him to a school in London as a day-boy. They had sent Charles to Hill House in Knightsbridge partly to get him used gradually to being away from the home atmosphere before he went away as a boarder to a preparatory school. But Andrew needed no such careful weaning. He was eager to get out into the world. In addition the Queen and Prince Philip had been worried about the activities of the press, especially photographers, when Charles had been at Hill

Andrew enjoyed being a member of 1st Marylebone Cub Scout pack which met regularly in the grounds of Buckingham Palace.

Moving at the double, Andrew attends his last meeting of the Cub pack at Buckingham Palace. He was off shortly to his prep school, Heatherdown, near Ascot.

House in the centre of London. It was agreed, however, that it would probably be best all round if he went away to school when he was eight in 1968. The news was received with a certain amount of relief by those who had to deal with him every day. Meanwhile to work off some of his energy he joined a class of boys of around his own age who did gymnastics, athletics and rudimentary team games at Burton's Court, a pleasant cricket ground used by the Brigade of Guards in front of the Royal Hospital, the Army Pensioners' home in Chelsea.

They were happy years for the family. Prince Charles, who was eighteen at the end of 1968, had come back from his six months at Timbertop in Australia a changed young man, self-confident and outward-looking. The months in the outback camp of the Geelong Grammar School of Melbourne had given him just the right atmosphere to shake off the self-consciousness that had concealed his potential. 'The most wonderful experience I've ever had I think,' he said some years later. He had already taken his O-levels and was going back for another year to Gordonstoun to take A-levels and then, if all was well, going on to Cambridge. The change in Charles brought pleasure to the Queen and Prince Philip – perhaps especially to Prince Philip, who felt that he had finally been justified in being tough with his son and making him endure the unhappy years at Cheam and Gordonstoun.

Anne was enjoying herself at Benenden and doing as much riding as she could. By now she was competing in Pony Club horse trials, gymkhanas and hunter trials. She was fond of all her brothers in her brusque way, enjoyed their company and admitted, 'I'm delighted I did not have a sister.'

In spite of all her duties the Queen managed to spend quite a lot of time with her children. Apart from their love for her as their mother they stood a little in awe of her because they realized as they grew up that, however much she might relax with them, she was the Queen. In the long weeks at Balmoral, however, the outside world seemed a long way away and the Queen could spend most of her time with the family, walking, riding, picnicking, playing Scrabble and doing jigsaw puzzles. The whole family looked forward to Balmoral and were a little sad when the time came to pack up and face the world again.

In the autumn of 1968 Andrew was sent away to preparatory school. The choice was Heatherdown near Ascot, not far from Windsor. It did not have the prestige of Cheam which Charles and his father had attended, but it was expensive, exclusive and a large number of its boys went on to Eton. Andrew had no problem settling in and was soon known by the staff as one of the rowdier boys.

During the holidays, until the spring of 1969, he got to know what it was like to be surrounded by television cameras and their crews. With the rest of the family he was involved in the making of a film about its activities at work and play. It was a joint venture by the BBC and ITV and filming took place in over a hundred and

Prince Charles and Princess Anne organizing a family group on Christmas morning at Windsor. From left to right: Lady Sarah Armstrong-Jones, daughter of Princess Margaret and Lord Snowdon; James Ogilvy, son of Princess Alexandra and the Hon. Angus Ogilvy; the Earl of St Andrews, son of the Duke and Duchess of Kent; Lady Helen Windsor, their daughter; Viscount Linley, son of the Snowdons; Prince Andrew; Marina Ogilvy and Prince Edward.

The Queen takes Andrew, now eight, and Edward, four, to see their father play polo at Smith's Lawn, Windsor.

Andrew had just been yachting with his father, Prince Philip, at the Cowes Regatta. Princess Anne and Prince Edward are with them on the royal train en route for the customary holiday at Balmoral.

fifty locations. Finally it was cut to run for one hour fifty minutes, given the title of *Royal Family* and first put on the air at the end of June 1969, a week before the investiture of Prince Charles as Prince of Wales on 1 July at Caernarvon Castle. Andrew did not have to do much except enjoy himself and be reasonably tidy and obedient when he was in group scenes, but being almost entirely unselfconscious he came across as a lively, cheerful boy with a touch of the daredevil in his glance.

On its first showing the film was seen by twenty-three million people. It was repeated a week later and seen by fifteen million, of whom six million had already seen the first showing. Shorter versions were sold to many countries overseas. It was a great success, especially in Canada, Australia and New Zealand and had a very rewarding coverage in the United States.

Charles's investiture, which Andrew had to be content to watch on television, turned out a triumph in spite of a very unpleasant background of bombs and sabotage by Welsh Nationalist extremists. As a relief the Queen organized a family trip abroad in the royal yacht with all her children before the Balmoral holiday.

The family embarked at Hull after the Queen had paid an official visit to the city. They sailed up to the Shetland Islands and then crossed the North Sea to Norway to spend a few days as guests of King Olav, a relative of both the Queen and Prince Philip. It was a splendid trip. They were met by the King at Bergen and then sailed several hundred miles up the coast, calling at Andalnes and Molde and then making their way up the great Fjord to Trondheim. The scenery is magnificent, at times forbidding, and impressive enough to leave its mark on Andrew even if he was only nine.

Charles was twenty-one on 14 November that year and Anne was nineteen on 15 August. Charles had another year at Cambridge before he took his degree. Anne was not going to university and was already carrying out official engagements whilst carrying on with her riding in a serious, professional way. The two eldest children of the Queen and Prince Philip were grown up.

But Andrew found himself the leader of a younger generation of the royal family. There is a delightful photograph taken at Windsor Castle on Christmas Day 1969 which shows the new brood – and they look a lively, interesting group of children.

Lord St Andrews, who was two years younger than Andrew, was to join him later at Heatherdown. Edward had started classes at Buckingham Palace with Lady Sarah Armstrong-Jones and James Ogilvy. They had a new governess, for Miss Peebles had died shortly after Andrew went away to school and was replaced by Miss Lavinia Keppel who was of the same family as Alice Keppel, the mistress of King Edward VII.

The IRA terrorists' activities which had broken out in Ulster in 1969 spread to

England and in 1971 affected the life of Prince Andrew at Heatherdown. The Special Branch of the police learned at the end of 1970 that the IRA had laid plans to kidnap Lord St Andrews, who had by now started at Heatherdown, and hold him as hostage for the release of two of its members who were being held in prison. The information was somewhat imprecise and there was official concern that Prince Andrew might also be at risk.

At the beginning of January a full-scale police operation was put into action. There were rigorous searches of houses and business premises known to be occupied by IRA sympathizers in Ulster, the Midlands and the north of England. When the eighty boarders returned after the Christmas holidays they found that detectives were carefully screening the thirty acres of gardens and playing-fields. Both Andrew and Lord St Andrews found their movements restricted as Special Branch officers mounted a 24-hour guard over them.

Mr James Edwards, the headmaster, and his wife, Barbara, tried hard to preserve an atmosphere of calm, but it was not an easy time for them and the staff. The boys took it all as a great joke, a cops and robbers story happening in their midst. But the reality was that there was a definite risk and the IRA were both skilled and ruthless.

Precautions were gradually relaxed as the police believed the danger receded. But guards were always around as long as Andrew and Lord St Andrews were at the school. When Charles had been at Cheam the security problem had been to protect him from photographers. The threat at Heatherdown was far more dangerous.

Andrew at this time joined a Scouts group which was formed at Heatherdown. He enjoyed wearing the uniform of mushroom-coloured trousers, green shirt and beret but he enjoyed the activities even more; he shared with his family a love of the countryside, accepted bad weather cheerfully and responsibility in an easy manner.

Like other schools, Heatherdown sent parties of boys on outings to London to visit museums and places of educational value. In March Andrew was one of a group that was given a tour of the Natural History Museum in South Kensington. While they were going round the exhibits they were set on by three youths from the East End. Andrew was not involved in the fight but two Heatherdown boys were hurt before Andrew's detective and attendants tackled the youths. They were taken before Scotland Yard's juvenile liaison bureau and given a severe warning. It was not a serious incident but it gave the Heatherdown boys, including Andrew, a slight intimation that the world outside their protected domain could have a rough and hostile aspect.

During the Easter holidays Andrew went with the rest of the royal family to watch Princess Anne competing in the Three-Day Event at Badminton, one of the toughest equestrian competitions in the world. Anne had tried desperately hard to be able to qualify and finally succeeded. Badminton, a postwar development made possible by the Duke of Beaufort, a relative of the Queen and Master of the Queen's Horse, had become to horse trials what Wimbledon is to tennis or Henley to rowing. The Queen nearly always managed to attend, often with the Queen Mother and Princess Margaret. They stayed with the Duke of Beaufort and their presence made it a social as well as a sporting occasion.

Against top-class competition, both British and international, Anne came fifth out of forty-eight in the Three-Day Event. It was a great achievement which repaid her constant hard work. The whole family was delighted and Andrew, who is as competitive as his sister, admired her as she tackled the cross-country with its daunting thirty-one obstacles on the second day.

They are a closely-knit family, sharing each other's triumphs and disappointments, and 1971 was Anne's year of triumph. She went on to Burghley in September and won the Raleigh Trophy as Individual European Three-Day Event Champion. As a final accolade she was voted Sportswoman of the Year. Her character, however, did not change. She was twenty-one that year and it would have been natural for her to have a great party just as Charles had had on his twenty-first. But she didn't want one, disliking all the fuss and bother. So, to vary the Balmoral holiday, the family sailed up in *Britannia* to Thurso on the north coast of Scotland where the Queen Mother has a romantic summer home, the Castle of Mey. Anne was perfectly content to have her birthday there with just the family around her – her grandmother, parents and brothers Charles, Andrew and Edward.

Andrew had reason also to be proud of his brother Charles this year. After taking his degree at Cambridge he joined the RAF for an advanced flying course – he had already learned to fly – and got his wings with ease. He then went on to the Royal Naval College at Dartmouth for a crash course before going to sea as an acting sub-lieutenant in the guided missile destroyer *Norfolk* for a five-week exercise in the Mediterranean. Mingled with Andrew's pride a certain envy would have been natural, but his father could cheer him up by telling him his turn would come.

His younger brother Edward had been sent as a day-boy to Gibbs, a preparatory school in Kensington. He was a quiet boy who gave no trouble and it was thought he would settle in easily with the other boys. His cousin, James Ogilvy, was also sent to the same school to keep him company.

At Christmas Andrew was able to see himself on television in the Queen's Christmas message. The Queen wanted to give a family touch with her two younger sons. They were shown turning over the pages of an album of old family photographs, the Queen describing to her sons their forebears of four generations.

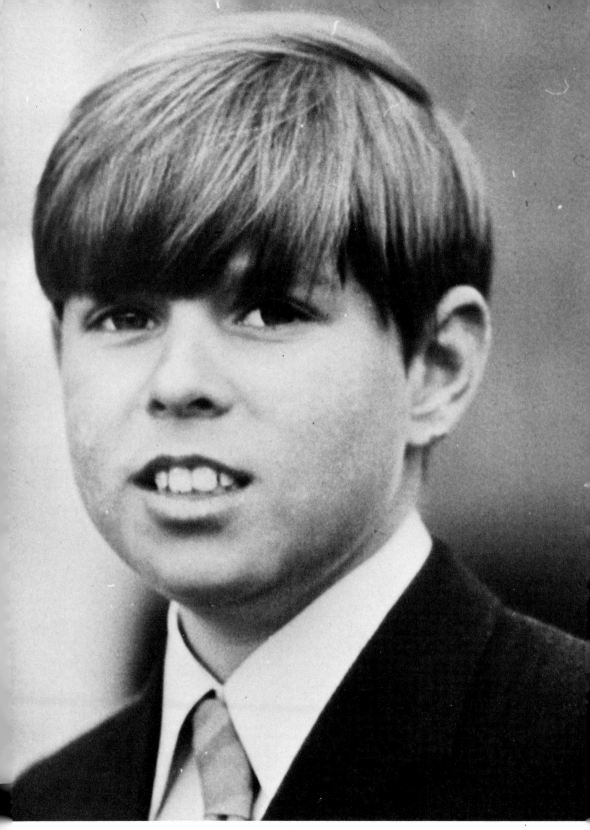

Andrew joins his prep school, Heatherdown. He looked forward to the rough and tumble of school.

It was skilfully produced and Andrew showed no signs of restlessness as great-grandparents and great-great-grandparents were reviewed.

The pattern of Andrew's life did not change much in the following year. Before going up to Balmoral in 1972 he was seen at the nets at Lord's being coached by the former Glamorgan player, Len Muncer, and was judged to have the promise of being a good cricketer. He went out on the grouse moors later in the year with his father and helped to retrieve game, but already he wanted to have his own gun. During the Christmas holidays the Bishop of Norwich, the Rt Rev. Maurice Wood, who often preached at the church in Sandringham and was a friend of the family, took Andrew to a League Cup match between Norwich and Chelsea. Mark Phillips was one of the guests at Sandringham that year and Fleet Street was already predicting he would be marrying Princess Anne – but this was strongly denied two months later in March 1973. Andrew was at Badminton in April and watched both Anne and Mark Phillips competing. Then on 29 May it was finally announced that his sister and Mark were engaged and would marry in Westminster Abbey on 14 November.

There was another announceent on 29 May. It was that Andrew, who was finishing at Heatherdown, would be going to Gordonstoun in the steps of his father and elder brother.

4

The Old School Ties

The school of Gordonstoun is centred on a stone-built country house not far from the Moray Firth in north-east Scotland. It is bleak country open to the storms of the North Sea, but has a rugged beauty. The hard climate and the loneliness breed a tough people to whom Edinburgh is as remote as London. It was here that Kurt Hahn, a Jewish exile from Nazi Germany, was given an opportunity to create a school based on the same ideals and practice as the one he had founded in Salem in south Germany soon after the First World War in the early twenties.

Hahn was a visionary, but it is doubtful that even he could have foreseen in his most prophetic moods that this school in a lonely, almost desolate corner of Scotland would educate the husband of Queen Elizabeth II and their three sons – Charles, heir to the throne, Andrew and, in time, Edward. It is a most extraordinary story.

Hahn was an able scholar, who studied at four German universities before coming to England to spend some time at Christchurch College, Oxford. Many of the undergraduates had come up from Eton and Hahn was fascinated by their easy manner of superiority. And at Oxford he was influenced by Plato's *Republic*, that vision of an ideal state ruled by a specially educated group of guardians. Hahn returned to Germany and during the First World War he served his country as an expert adviser on the English. At the end of the war he was private secretary to Prince Maximilian of Baden, the last Imperial Chancellor, and when Prince Max retreated to his country estate at Salem to write his memoirs Hahn went too to help him.

It was in the circle at Salem that Hahn was able to put forward his views on education. He thought that higher German education had relied on rigid discipline too greatly, so that the young grew up to obey blindly and not to think for themselves in a crisis. He also thought that the privileged young had been brought up as a caste apart with little or no understanding of the rest of the community. He developed his own theory of a better education, considerably influenced by what he had seen of the British public school system epitomized by Eton. To his mind it was based on a large measure of self-discipline. But, above all, Hahn preached

Plato's ideas on education: to produce an ideal state depended on the education of a ruling class, the Guardians, men and women almost godlike in their selflessness and dedication to the welfare of the state, exercising power with even-handed justice.

Prince Maximilian was impressed. He told Hahn he would help him start a pilot scheme in one of the adjoining buildings of Salem. That was the beginning of an educational system that has influenced countries throughout the world but nowhere more than Britain.

Prince Max, whose wife Marie-Louise of Hanover was a descendant of George III of England, sent his eldest son, Prince Berthold, as one of the first twenty pupils, who were indeed drawn mainly from other aristocratic families with a few, like the son of the innkeeper at Salem, from ordinary backgrounds. Prince Berthold was later to marry Prince Philip's sister, Theodora. It was one of Hahn's principles that a number of pupils from humble families should be given scholarships to widen the background of the privileged and give them an understanding of other classes.

Life at Salem was austere with cold showers in the morning and few comforts. The book learning was there, but not stressed. In sports the emphasis was on gymnastics, athletics, including javelin-throwing (as with the ancient Greeks), and hockey. There were arduous walks in the country and on the hills. Music (again as with the Greeks) was encouraged. There were periods of enforced rest and meditation. One of the most important aspects in Hahn's system was community work. There was work in the kitchen garden, a fire engine was acquired to help the local brigade. Later there was life-saving on Lake Constance and mountain rescue teams. Internal discipline was maintained by the Guardian (headboy) and the helpers (a Platonic term corresponding to English prefects). Punishment was enforced by homilies, deprivation of privileges and, in extreme cases, by expulsion.

To inculcate self-discipline, each pupil was provided with a book in which were headings covering all the daily duties from cold shower to co-operation. It was for the pupil to examine himself and record his own failings.

This Hahn system, a curious hybrid of German and British traditions and ancient Greek idealism, caught on. The school flourished; satellites were formed in the neighbourhood, including Lake Constance with its sailing facilities; other schools in Germany were influenced.

Hahn's personality had much to do with the success. He inspired enthusiasm and trust. He had enormous self-confidence so that he could justify to himself, if not always to everyone else, contradictions in his thinking. He was that rare man, a practical idealist.

There were other reasons for the success of the school. Germany was down-

Andrew is the tallest boy in a loose scrum (*top*). Competitive from an early age, he carefully judges the distance for a practice place-kick (*above*).

and-out and, as the news spread that a man had formed a school where a new breed of Germans was being produced, self-confident, self-disciplined and forward-looking, there was a ready response. For the princely families it was comforting that their sons – and some daughters – would be brought up among friends and relatives under the patronage of the House of Baden. For the rich industrialists and bankers, although the Germans are not so naturally snobbish as the British, it was agreeable that their offspring should be educated with the children of the old nobility. To that extent Salem was becoming similar to Eton, although Hahn made the rich pay for the privilege by subsidizing the intake of those who could not afford the full fees. And as the fame of Salem spread, the rich expatriate German families who had done well, especially in South America, sent their children back to be educated by Hahn and to preserve their German culture.

But Hitler came to power in 1933, when Prince Philip was a pupil at Salem, and the school disintegrated. Some of the boys were Nazis and went around parading the swastika and sneering at Hahn, the Jew. At first Hahn had listened to Hitler's promises to restore Germany to greatness. But now he appreciated the evils of Nazism, and bravely and openly protested against a particularly brutal murder by Nazi thugs. He wrote to the old boys of Salem: 'It is a question now in Germany of its Christian morality, its reputation, its soldierly honour: Salem cannot remain neutral. I call on all members of the Salem Association who are active in the SA or the ss to terminate their allegiance either to Hitler or to Salem.'

It was not long before Salem was taken over by the Nazis and Hahn arrested. Fortunately his friends in Germany were still powerful and high-level appeals were made in Britain. The headmaster of Eton, the Archbishop of Canterbury, John Buchan (later Lord Tweedsmuir), author and proconsul, made, with others, representations to the British Government and Hahn was released and with overwhelming sadness left the country he loved so deeply and came to Britain as a poor exile.

He was helped financially to set up Gordonstoun to be run on his principles. Prince Philip was one of the first pupils to follow him there. Not many others came from Salem. Most of them came from families which came to terms with the Hitler regime. A large number of the boys became officers in the army which for some time preserved a measure of independence whilst appreciating its new power as the instrument of German aggression.

When Britain and France went to war in 1939 the irrepressible Hahn tried to insinuate himself into the corridors of power in Whitehall and play the same role in London as he had played in Berlin in the First World War. But Churchill and the men around him had no time for any Germans – even exiled Jews – unless they had valuable secrets. Hahn did not consider himself disloyal to Germany in wanting to serve Britain. He still hoped for a revolution in Germany which would overthrow Hitler. He had become, as so many exiles do, out of touch with the reality of the country he had left.

Gordonstoun was evacuated to Wales and managed to keep going in a modest way. With the defeat of Germany in 1945 Hahn was soon visiting that devastated country trying to establish old links and help where he could. In spite of the persecution of the Jews, the abasement of elementary values, the cult of violence, Germany still evoked sympathy in him as he saw her humbled and ruined.

But his life-work was to be in Britain. He became a christian and a British subject. The marriage of Prince Philip to the then Princess Elizabeth, heir to the throne, increased interest in Gordonstoun. Once more the school flourished and Prince Philip, who revered Hahn, did all he could to help – and it proved a great deal.

The Duke of Edinburgh's Award Scheme which spread to the Commonwealth was inspired by Gordonstoun thinking. Outward Bound courses for the young flourished, first of all here and then in many other countries, as school authorities and employers responded to Hahn's argument that a largely urbanized youth needed the tough challenge of the sea and the mountains. Schools were founded on Gordonstoun principles in Britain, Germany, the United States, Greece and Africa. Many other schools throughout the world established links with what was now the mother school, Gordonstoun, exchanging boys and teachers. In Wales an ambitious project came into being at St Donat's Castle, where a United World College was founded to train an international group of boys and girls of sixth-form levels before they went on to university. Similar colleges now exist in Singapore and Canada and others are projected. Lord Mountbatten was the first president and has now been succeeded by Prince Charles.

Before he died Hahn, in his youth a patriotic German, received honours from his adopted country. In 1953 Prince Philip, as Chancellor of the University of Edinburgh, conferred on him an honorary doctorate of law and in 1964 he was created a CBE. Hahn's life was one of astonishing achievement. His diagnosis of the challenge to modern teachers remained virtually unchanged over forty years:

The young to-day are surrounded by tempting declines – declines which affect the adult world – the decline of fitness, due to modern methods of moving about; decline of memory and imagination, due to the confused restlessness of modern life; decline of skill and care, due to the weakened tradition of craftsmanship; decline of self-discipline, due to stimulants and tranquillizers. Worst of all, the decline in compassion, due to the unseemly haste with which life is conducted.

These 'tempting declines' he wished, in some measure, to halt.

It was a noble ambition. The ideals are unexceptionable, doubts lurk in some quarters about the system, particularly the inspiration of Plato who despised democracy and admired the authoritarian regime of Sparta which had destroyed the freedom of his native Athens. However, few educationalists have sought so hard and so long to improve the quality of young men and women. Perhaps the schools he founded will produce a new breed of Siegfrieds and Brünhildes, self-disciplined, just and compassionate who will devote their lives not to personal gain but the service of mankind.

All in all, it could be said that postwar Gordonstoun has preserved the original framework of Salem as it was in 1920, with an inner core of princes and nobles of the old ruling Houses of Europe.

When Charles was finishing at his preparatory school, Cheam, there was a debate in the royal family where he should be sent for his further schooling. Prince Philip had no doubt that he should go to his old school, Gordonstoun. At first the Queen was undecided and some of her advisers were not enthusiastic about the Hahn system and would have preferred the heir to the throne to go to Eton, the traditional school of the nobility and the respectable rich. When the family was at Balmoral Philip drove the Queen over to Gordonstoun and extolled its virtues with the help of an enthusiastic staff. Apart from the arguments put forward by Philip there was another which was relevant. Eton is loosely organized in houses around the High Street of the town and wide open to the ingenuity of the press, particularly photographers. Gordonstoun is remote, centred round the main house and more easily guarded both against the press and more dangerous threats.

The upshot was that the Queen was convinced and Charles started at the school in May 1962. He ended up as guardian or head boy before he left in the summer of 1967 to go on to Cambridge. The Queen must have been satisfied with the result because there was no surprise when it was announced in 1973 that Prince Andrew would be going to Gordonstoun.

The Queen's decision to send all three of her sons to Gordonstoun (for in due course Prince Edward also joined the school) was probably not entirely due to the persuasions of Prince Philip, although she respects his natural rights as father. The British royal house is German in origin and has remained by marriage predominantly so. But it does not stop there. The royal houses of Europe, whatever the country, were predominantly German. Even the proud House of Romanov had been German since Catherine the Great, who was a German princess.

All these families are inextricably related. Many monarchies have fallen, but the British Crown remains secure, popular and of worldwide prestige. Queen Elizabeth II is, in a way, the head of a great family and the other royal houses, whether they still reign or not, look up to her.

It is, therefore, understandable that the Queen should look with a favourable eye on a school whose patron was the Margrave of Baden, which is closely connected with the House of Hanover and which attracts relatives of the royal family, both close and distant. Eton has its nobility, but Gordonstoun has its royalty, even if exiled.

Since Charles, followed by Andrew and Edward, have gone to Gordonstoun, the school, including masters and pupils has, as it were, been moulded to provide a background which Prince Philip believes is appropriate for the education, academic, physical and social, of the next generation of the House of Windsor. Eton, steeped in its own traditions, would never have allowed itself to be moulded even by the presence of royal princes. It would have considered that they would be wise to mould themselves to its own background.

5

Raving to Go

It might not be correct to say that Heatherdown was glad to see the back of Andrew, but there was a certain relief and gratitude that nothing irreparable had happened. Andrew could be diligent at his books and domestic chores, turn out on time for games and be polite to everyone. Then a mood would come over him and he would be aggressive, rude and obstinate. The mood is not unknown in preparatory schools and the staff would have known how to deal with it if they had been dealing with one of the other pupils. But in the case of Prince Andrew it involved discussions with the headmaster and the creation of tension. It was not an easy time for anyone – apart from the security aspect.

However, Andrew marched away with a smile and looked forward to the summer holidays before he tackled Gordonstoun. As well as coaching in cricket he was given tennis lessons by Dan Maskell, the ex-Wimbledon player and BBC commentator, went swimming and began to amuse himself, but not his family, with practical jokes. There were cushions which made rude noises when sat upon, hairy hands and stink-bombs. He climbed on the roof of Buckingham Palace and fiddled around with the TV aerials, upsetting reception. He got hold of some large bottles of bath essence, poured them into the swimming-pool at Windsor Castle and stirred up the water until it was covered with foam just before the family was going for a dip. As his mother admitted somewhat ruefully at this time, 'He is not always a little ray of sunshine about the home!'

Andrew was, in fact, only following in the family tradition. His elder brother, Charles had been a late developer and left it until he joined the Navy to develop a taste for practical jokes, suddenly appearing out of a large cardboard container in the wardroom and pelting his fellow-officers with custard tarts or gooey cakes, breaking off to direct jets of soda water from a supply of siphons.

In August 1973 Andrew joined his father and younger brother at Cowes where they stayed on the royal yacht. This year his father borrowed *Yeoman* XIX from the rich patron of yachting, Owen Aisher, to compete in the Britannia Cup race. Conditions were very fresh offshore, but Andrew looked as if he was enjoying every minute of it as he clung to the guard-rails watching his father at the helm and an expert crew handling the beautiful ocean-racer.

Andrew, sitting alongside his younger brother, Edward, drives along the Mall with the Queen Mother to watch his mother at the Queen's Birthday Parade on 10 June 1973.

One of the few formal photographs taken of Prince Andrew with his younger brother, Prince Edward.

Then it was up to Balmoral where Andrew was out on the grouse moors with his father and trying his hand with a gun. But this year the calm of the family holiday was somewhat disturbed by the preparations for Anne's wedding on 14 November. A royal wedding may look glamorous finally on the TV screens, but the preparations are so intricate that excitement competes with weariness. In addition Anne was going with her father and Mark Phillips to Kiev in Russia at the beginning of September to take part in the European Horse Trials Championship. Apart from the object of the visit it was something of a milestone for the British royal family to set foot in Soviet Russia.

For Andrew, however, it was time to start at Gordonstoun, but he knew he would be given leave to come down to London for his sister's marriage.

Since Charles had left in 1967, six years previously, the school had changed somewhat. A new man, Mr John Kempe, was in charge and he commented, 'Just after Prince Charles left a new headmaster – myself – came to the school with new ideas.'

The school had had to change in certain respects to survive. Parents, originally attracted by the royal patronage, had in some cases been disillusioned. Academic results were poor in comparison with many public schools and qualifications, as well as connections, were needed in the modern world. Some boys had just not been able to endure the moral fervour and the austerities and had been taken away.

But, even more important, all public schools, however ancient and tied to tradition, were changing in response to a climate of opinion which, for good or for bad, was modifying society at all levels. In Britain 'the permissive society' burgeoned in the sixties and swept all before it.

So far as education was concerned old disciplines were relaxed and emphasis placed on friendly co-operation between master and pupil. Girls arrived in many of the most prestigious schools and were soon admitted to Oxford and Cambridge colleges which had been for many centuries male preserves. Their presence solved some problems and created others. Homosexuality caused by the absence of the other sex rather than natural inclination tended to disappear. The inhibiting shyness in associating with the other sex caused by segregation became less of an English disease. On the other hand propinquity and the availability of contraception made sex casual and love a less likely experience. But regrets for the past were otiose; new forms of relationships between the sexes were being formed which would permanently change the texture of society.

At Gordonstoun the admission of girls was no more than a return to Hahn's original practice when Salem was founded. The year before Andrew arrived thirty girls had been admitted and as many again were to join the following year. But this was only one aspect of the changes made at the school. Mr Kempe commented: 'Whatever the school's reputation was or is, it is not an extremely Spartan school. We have central heating and a swimming-pool heated to seventy-five degrees.' It was no longer compulsory to take a cold shower in winter. Academic standards were raised to fit the pupils for university or professional careers. Sports were organized on a more orthodox basis with greater emphasis placed on rugby football and cricket for the boys.

It would be misleading, however, to think that the spirit of Hahn did not still hover over the school. *'Plus est en vous'* [there is more in you] than you think, was still the school motto and the spirit of moral and physical endeavour was still there. Communal activity was still an essential theme – even to a fire-engine, as at prewar Salem, which was a source of fun to the pupils, but not regarded as an unmixed blessing by the local fire-brigade. There was a coastguard service and life-saving teams. There were enough mountains around to justify skilled mountain rescue teams. There was a handsome ketch, *Sea Spirit*, to man at sea and many smaller craft for inshore work. So far as this mountain and sea activity was concerned Mr Kempe was right when he said that the Gordonstoun system had been copied by many schools. It was part fun and part a challenge and strengthened the character of all who took part, whereas for most young people their role in team games was to provide a background to those who shone.

Prince Andrew arrived at Gordonstoun full of bounce. His attitude of 'I am the prince' did not go down at all well with the other boys. They bided their time, saw how the land lay with the masters and then started to counter-attack by 'taking the mickey' mercilessly. Andrew realized he was up against tougher opposition than at Heatherdown, modified his manner and started to be accepted. But he was not a boy to change, he bided his time in turn: it was only a tactic of *reculer pour mieux sauter*.

His term was interrupted by leave to attend his sister's wedding. The Queen sent up one of the royal aircraft to fetch him, and he was soon immersed in the family pleasure and the public pageantry. Charles was on leave from the Navy. Edward, all dressed up in court uniform with a jabot, was to be Anne's page and travelled to Westminster Abbey in a coach with Lady Sarah Armstrong-Jones who was the only bridesmaid.

The Queen gave a great dinner-party, followed by an immense reception before the day. A large contingent of relatives arrived from Europe to give a royal atmosphere, in contrast to the more down-to-earth relatives of Mark Phillips and the friends made by Anne in the show-jumping world. The ceremony in Westminster Abbey was one of colourful splendour and seen by countless millions on television screens then and later. Troops lined the processional way; there were cheering crowds; appearances on the balcony at Buckingham Palace and finally a wedding breakfast for 130 guests ending with traditional waves, kisses, tears and laughter as the couple drove off on the first stage of a magnificent honeymoon on the royal yacht to the West Indies and beyond.

Andrew had a great time, especially as he had always been fond of his sister; her no-nonsense, at times brusque, attitude found a response in him. She was a chum rather than an elder sister.

In the new year, 1974, Andrew was tackling Gordonstoun again. The masters found they were dealing with an intelligent boy who was willing to apply himself to his books. It was not that he was more intelligent than Charles, but he had self-confidence and his reactions were swifter. He did not suffer from the mental block that had made mathematics such a grind for both Charles and Anne. He made a few friends with whom he shared a birthday cake in February, but there were no great festivities, for Andrew, like Charles before him, was restricted in pocket-money to a bare minimum.

It was in this term that Andrew was called to the headmaster's study to be given some disturbing news about his sister Anne. A daring attempt had been made to kidnap her as she was being driven back to Buckingham Palace with her husband after attending a film-show. At 7.40 p.m. on 20 March 1974 a car turned sharply in front of the royal car as it approached the Palace from the Mall and forced it to stop. The driver of the blocking car came over and opened the car door nearest to Anne and told her to get out. He had a revolver in his hand and another in reserve. In the ensuing struggle the Princess's detective, James Beaton, was shot three times; the royal driver was shot, so were a police constable who ran over to the scene and a journalist who was passing by chance and tried to help. Finally the man was overpowered. The attacker was Ian Ball, twenty-six, a somewhat eccentric man operating on his own. He had planned the attempt with great skill and had rented a hideaway house near Sandburst where Anne had been living since Mark Phillips had been appointed an instructor at the Royal Military Academy there.

When Anne got back to the Palace, 'very thankful to be in one piece', as she said, she put through a call to her parents who were in Indonesia and to Charles whose ship, HMS *Jupiter*, was visiting Acapulco in Mexico. Andrew also spoke to his sister after he had been told the news.

The incident caused a great stir in Britain and, indeed, throughout the world. There had been for some time an upsurge of terrorism on an international scale. Palestinian Arabs were attacking Jews. The Baader-Meinhof gang in Germany and the Red Brigades in Italy were well-organized and ruthless killers. In Britain the IRA had spread its activities from Ulster to England.

Ian Ball was found insane at his trial and sent to a mental hospital for surveillance 'without limit of time'. But his attempt had shown gaps in police

The horse trials at Badminton, which the royal family attends every year, partly because Princess Anne has been a notable competitor. Here Andrew is with his mother, the Queen, his aunt, Princess Margaret and his elder brother, Prince Charles (partly concealed). With them is the Duke of Beaufort, with whom the family stay at Badminton.

Andrew standing beside the Duke of Beaufort at Badminton. With him is a contingent of his cousins. From left to right: Lady Helen Windsor; Lady Sarah Armstrong-Jones; the Earl of St Andrews and Viscount Linley.

security. More elaborate precautions had to be taken. Up at Gordonstoun it was realized that, though the school was in a remote area of the Highlands, there was no guarantee of safety against skilled plotting. So, as at Heatherdown, Andrew found himself closely watched. The staff sighed at the restrictions on the school, and hoped for the best.

In the spring Andrew went with the family to watch Anne and Mark Phillips riding at Badminton, went back for the summer term and thoroughly enjoyed his cricket this year for he was developing as a good all-rounder. In August the Queen and Prince Philip organized another trip in the *Britannia* en route for Balmoral. With Andrew were Edward and Princess Margaret's two children, Viscount Linley and Lady Sarah. The North Sea oilfields were being developed now and Aberdeen, formerly a prim granite city with a famous university, was being transformed into an operating base, buzzing with helicopters, its harbour filled with supply vessels and its hotels and bars booming as the oilmen enjoyed their hard-earned leaves with girls who had heard of the new wealth. The *Britannia* sailed to Nigg Bay where a £50-million oil platform was nearing completion for use in British Petroleum's Forties Field. It was an impressive sight not only for Andrew and the other youngsters. Philip, with his scientific bent, was full of questions. The Queen knew that self-sufficiency in oil by 1980, which now seemed likely, would give Britain a chance to halt its industrial decline and equip the industries of the future – the future of her children and everybody else's.

At Balmoral, apart from the picnics on the hills, swimming, shooting and fishing, Andrew was this year allowed to start learning to drive on the private roads of the estate. Charles even let him have a go in the driving seat of his own Aston Martin. But Andrew broke off his family holiday to go to France for three weeks in a party of fifteen Gordonstoun boys.

It was an exchange visit with the Caousou Jesuit College near Toulouse in the south-east of France not far from the Pyrenees. Security precautions were very strict. Special Branch men went over from England and were joined by French detectives. There was no mention of the visit in the British press until it was over. Even the French press, normally less willing to accept government orders than Fleet Street, kept its silence and it was not until Andrew was safely back in England that it was learned that he had told a reporter who managed to glimpse him on his arrival, 'My name is Andrew Edwards. My father is a gentleman farmer and my mother does not work.' For a fourteen-year-old it was quite a cleverly contrived piece of irony!

During the visit there were French lessons, but the object of the trip was for the boys to hear French being spoken and to try to improve their own accents. There was a soccer match with the French boys: Gordonstoun lost, although Andrew scored a goal. There was a lot of sightseeing and there were always excellent guides to show the boys round.

Toulouse, and its surroundings, was an interesting choice for a visit. The city is ancient, but in the postwar renaissance of France inspired by de Gaulle it has become the centre for great new industries and is now the fourth largest town in France. It is the centre of the aircraft industry and the French Concordes are built there, providing an absorbing tour for Andrew and the rest of the Gordonstoun party. Old Toulouse is built of rose-red brick along the Garonne, has nearly a hundred Renaissance houses, ancient churches and a cathedral, and a flourishing university. For Andrew, whose family traces its descent back to William the Conqueror, the history of the city was worth attention. The Counts of Toulouse were the greatest dynasty of southern France in the feudal period and ruled great areas of the country. That remarkable woman, Eleanor of Aquitaine, who married Henry II of England and brought with her a large slice of France, was related to a Count of Toulouse.

For security reasons Andrew stayed with a doctor and his family in one of the prosperous suburbs of Toulouse. He was charming to them, but one of the teachers exclaimed with relief when he left, '*Mon Dieu*, he was certainly a handful!'

He was proving a handful back at Gordonstoun. In a dormitory fight he got a crack on the head which put him into hospital for a couple of days. One of his masters commented around this time, 'He's a very tough and independent fellow. He has no time for sycophants. He's good – just as good – with verbalistics as he is with his fists.'

Andrew was growing rapidly now (he would be nearly six feet, taller than most of the family). He was blonde, with vivid blue eyes and a charm which even the flatterers qualified with the adjective 'aggressive'. He resembled his father at the same age, according to some who should have known. Philip was pleased and proud of Andrew commenting with a grin, 'He's a natural boss'. He was also by now appreciating the presence of the girls at school. Charles who remembered Gordonstoun without any feminine attractions said his brother was already appreciating the innovation; 'He's enjoying himself immensely!'

After Christmas at Windsor the family went to Sandringham for the usual holiday, but not this time to the big house. It was being modernized by the Queen at a cost of £200,000 and the workmen were in. But a large farmhouse on the estate, Wood Farm, had been made ready. As it happened, the work on the big house was suspended in the New Year. The Queen was going to have to ask Parliament for a large increase in the Civil List to make up for the galloping inflation which was afflicting the country. Although Sandringham is owned by the family and the modernization costs would be found out of the Queen's private fortune, it was thought to be prudent not to be seen spending such a large sum at

The Queen and Prince Philip enjoy a joke with their two younger sons, Andrew and Edward, in the grounds of Buckingham Palace.

that time. The increase in the Civil List went through and a few years later, when economic conditions were better, Sandringham was restored.

However, although Andrew was negotiating for an increase in his £10 a term pocket-money – also hit by rising prices – he was unconcerned as yet about national affairs. What probably did interest him this holiday was the report by Charles on his three-month training as a naval helicopter pilot. Andrew envied him – just as he envied him being able to talk about his long experience as a pilot, for Charles had first started to learn to fly at Cambridge when he was nineteen. The trouble was that Andrew was impatient to go out and do everything, forgetting that he was over eleven years younger than his brother.

In the spring of 1975, soon after Andrew's fifteenth birthday, Audrey Whiting, who has been writing with insight about the royal family for many years, had an article published in the *Sunday Mirror* about him. She said he was being groomed as 'the understudy'. She quoted a court official as saying:

In this modern age we cannot close our eyes to the fact that Charles could have a fatal accident. He could easily have been killed when a ball grazed his chin when he was playing polo. Twice he has been involved in forced helicopter landings and there were also one or two minor incidents when he was on an Army Commando course. Through no fault of his own when he was driving his own car he had three near misses. This is why Prince Andrew, under the direction of his parents and their close advisers, is having a much broader and in many ways tougher upbringing and education than Prince Charles ever experienced.

Andrew was certainly experiencing a broader education than his brother Charles had ever had at Gordonstoun. In response to the trend of the day a disco evening was now allowed every other week at the school. It is best not to think what Kurt Hahn, that austere man with high principles, would have thought of the innovation.

At the disco Andrew was soon showing the old Hanoverian gusto. 'He's a great dancer,' said one fourteen-year-old girl. 'I've danced with him many times. But,' she added a little sadly, 'he dances with a lot of girls. Just when you think you are getting somewhere with him he goes off with another girl. I suppose it's for the best really. If he ever got stuck with one girl, she would be eaten alive!' It seems, however, that the chances of a secret date were remote, because he was so closely shadowed. 'Andy doesn't seem to notice, but I found it most distracting when we used to go about together,' said the disconsolate girl. 'It's a real passion-killer, if you'll excuse the phrase.' No wonder that Wendy Henry was able to apostrophize him in the *News of The World* as, 'Happy Andy! The dishy prince who's really raving to go!'

There was still, however, a sterner side to the old school. Later in the year he was one of the crew that sailed the school ketch, *Sea Spirit*, round Scotland in rough weather. When they reached Oban on the west coast Andrew broke away with his detective and made for the Royal Hotel and asked the manager if he could have the use of a bathroom to tidy up. 'I didn't charge him,' said the manager, which was just as well; as Andrew is always broke, the detective would have had to dip into his wallet.

In July the Queen and Prince Philip went to Gordonstoun to take part in end-of-school-year ceremonies and watched Andrew playing a minor role in a quite amusing farce, *Simple Spyman*. For the royal family amateur dramatics are not just a pastime; they are a useful preparation for its public role. There has always been a histrionic aspect of monarchy – the appearances in robes, splendid costumes and uniforms, the ritual gestures, the gracious speeches, all help to create the atmosphere of awe and excitement which is part of its popular function. The need for some degree of acting skill by the royal family has been increased by the advent of television. Inevitably its appearances are compared, even if unconsciously, with those of the professionals playing their dramatic roles.

The Queen Mother, conscious of the help some acting experience would give, arranged for Elizabeth and Margaret to take part in Christmas pantomimes when they were young. Margaret loved it all for she was a natural actress, but Elizabeth always needed a lot of coaxing. Elizabeth was still suffering from an embarrassing shyness when she married Prince Philip, but he helped her overcome it by sheer force of personality.

Both Charles's parents and his schoolmasters were glad when they found he was interested in dramatics at a time when he was still a somewhat withdrawn boy. When he was seventeen he took on the title role of *Macbeth*, worked hard at memorizing the long part, patiently listened to advice and gave a very creditable performance indeed in front of his parents. Later at Cambridge he was an enthusiastic member of the drama society at Trinity and appeared in sixteen of the forty sketches in its review, *Revulution*, including a monologue from a dustbin.

Andrew commented on amateur dramatics that he liked acting because he could pretend he was somebody else. 'I become bored with being myself and like taking on other roles.' He added, 'My brother [Charles] is far better at dramatics. I make a comedian of myself.' The remarks showed another side of Andrew's character. Under the breezy aggressiveness, there may well be inner tension resulting from a sense of insufficiency. As he was growing up he was also bound to realize the huge difference between being heir to the throne and a second son.

In the autumn, however, he seized an opportunity to do something neither his brother – nor his father, though an experienced pilot – had done. He went on a gliding course. He was a member of the Air Training Corps at school and gliding was encouraged among the senior boys. Andrew was only fifteen, but he got the permission of the school and his parents and had his first lesson in November. He

PRINCE ANDREW

had a first-class instructor, Flight-Lieutenant Peter Bullivant, who was a senior instructor at the Air Training Corps Central Gliding School, RAF. Andrew was soon in the air with him in a two-seater which was based at Milltown Airfield in Morayshire, not far from the school. Bullivant found him quite fearless and quick to learn. After the Christmas holidays Andrew carried on with the training enthusiastically and in July qualified for his ATC gliding proficiency wings by flying solo three four-minute circuits at Milltown.

It had been a good year for Andrew. In sport he was playing cricket in the First Eleven and he took six O-levels with no problems.

As soon as term was over in July Andrew was off on a wonderful trip which turned out to have a considerable influence on his development. He flew to Montreal to see the Olympic Games which his mother was opening on the seventeenth of the month. There was an extra excitement – his sister, Anne, had finally achieved her ambition and was riding in the British Equestrian Team.

The whole family was there to cheer her on. Charles had leave from the Navy where he was finishing his five years' service by commanding HMS *Bronington*, a 360-ton minehunter. Edward was on his summer holidays from school. As Philip stood by the Queen at the opening of the Games, he could reflect on his children with considerable satisfaction. The three eldest were already showing that they had inherited his determination and love of adventure.

The Queen had celebrated her fiftieth birthday two months before on 21 April, and Andrew had attended the great dinner and dance at Windsor Castle the evening before. In her reign she had enhanced the monarchy, and the affection of her subjects had deepened as year by year she calmly and quietly performed her duties with increasing skill.

At sixteen Andrew was old enough to realize he was a member of a very special family.

Andrew talks with the experts at the Badminton Horse Trials – his sister, Princess Anne, her husband, Captain Mark Phillips, and Allison Oliver, the well-known trainer of Anne's horses.

Above When he was fifteen Andrew went on a gliding course in the Air Training Corps at Gordonstoun. His instructor, Flight Lieutenant Peter Bullivant, described him as fearless and quick to learn.

Right Andrew had just completed his first solo glider flight. In July 1976, at the age of sixteen, he qualified for his glider proficiency wings.

6

The Challenge of Canada

Andrew arrived by air at Montreal on 16 July 1976 and then went by helicopter to the harbour where the royal yacht *Britannia* was moored on the St Lawrence and joined the Queen and Prince Philip aboard. They had had a busy time since he last saw them. The United States was this year celebrating the two-hundredth anniversary of its Independence from the British crown and the Queen had gone to Philadelphia, the seat of the revolution, and in a speech there said, 'We lost the American colonies because we lacked that statesmanship "to know the right time and manner of yielding what is impossible to keep".' Later, she and Philip had gone on to Washington where President Ford entertained them at a great banquet and dance in the White House. Finally they had flown up to Canada where the royal yacht was waiting and toured some of the western provinces before coming to Montreal to open the xxi Olympic Games of the modern era.

Princess Anne, as a competitor, had already arrived with her husband and they were living in the Olympic Village. Prince Charles and young Edward were to arrive in a couple of days. When the family was complete it would be the first time that they had all been abroad from Britain together in the same place.

When Andrew had a chance to look round he could not but have noticed the group of Canadian warships which guarded the royal yacht. They were not entirely a ceremonial guard of honour. Constant checks were made under water on the hull of the *Britannia* to make sure no explosives had been attached. Visitors and their belongings were carefully screened. They were sombre reminders that Montreal was the greatest city of the French-speaking province of Quebec and the centre of a great popular movement for separation from the rest of English-speaking Canada, with an extremist fringe which had resorted to violence. The Queen and her family faced a difficult task. According to a Gallup poll 65 per cent of French Canadians were opposed to the Queen coming to open the Games. The political leaders of Quebec were opposed to her visit because they felt it would undermine their separatist campaign and stress the federal unity of Canada. On the other hand, Pierre Trudeau, Prime Minister of Canada, was delighted that the

Queen and her family had come because he, son of a French-speaking father and an English-speaking mother, was doing his best to hold the country together and saw the royal visit as a means of helping his aim.

It is not an exaggeration to say that every member of the royal family had a diplomatic as well as a ceremonial part to play in this visit. Andrew, very mature for his sixteen years, soon showed he had just the right personality. He had not been there long before he was winning glowing approval with his youthful exuberance.

The Games needed some happy youthful exuberance for the atmosphere was beset with clouds. There had been shocking delays in completing the buildings due to industrial disputes and much was unfinished even on the opening day. The cost of holding the Games mounted to around £750 million and sorely taxed an already struggling Quebec community.

Security was so strict that it became burdensome. Parcels and people were scanned electronically so often that one visitor said, 'I've been X-rayed so much in this place I'm losing my sex drive!' The precautions were not due solely to the local Quebec problems. The authorities needed no reminding of the disaster at the Munich Games in 1972 when eleven Israeli athletes were killed by Palestinian gunmen. So for the 6,800 competitors there were 2,800 officials and 16,000 security men, many of them armed. In addition to all this the Queen, though Head of the Commonwealth, could do nothing to assuage the row that broke out between many African countries, some of them members of the Commonwealth, and New Zealand, one of its original members, because it was allowing a rugby team to tour South Africa. In all, twenty-nine of the original nations entered for the Games withdrew. To crown all there were accusations of drug-taking and cheating. Indeed Boris Onischenko, the captain of the Russian modern pentathlon team, was sent home after the discovery that he had illegal electrical connections to his fencing weapon that enabled him to 'score' points at will.

It is a tradition of the modern series of the Olympics to precede the Games with a great concert of music and song to honour the muses. The climax is reached when the orchestra plays the last movement of Beethoven's Ninth, the Choral Symphony, in which the massed choirs sing Schiller's *Ode to Joy* in the original German. Andrew, who has some German, was at the concert with his parents and may, like others, have wondered about the relevance in Montreal of the famous lines:

> *Alle Menschen werden Brüder*
> *Wo dein sanfter Flügel weilt.*
> [All men become brothers
> Where stays your gentle wing.]

63

Nevertheless, all was not misery at the Games – certainly not for Andrew. The Queen gave a glittering reception on board the *Britannia* with several hundred guests and Andrew was there looking very grown-up in his dinner-jacket. He stood by his parents at the opening ceremony in the enormous stadium and saw the torch-bearer run in to light the flame that would burn throughout the Games. He watched the march past of the national teams and there in the British team was his sister, Anne, wearing the rather fetching uniform for the British women which had finally been approved after much argument.

Andrew saw as much of the Games as he could – the choice was bewildering. He generally had a charming girl to guide him and at Kingston, where the yachting events took place, she was sixteen-year-old Sandi Jones, whom he was not to forget. One of the three gold medals Britain won was the Tornado Class Yachting Event, thanks to Reg White and John Osborn.

There was a visit to the Olympic Village to see how the competitors, among them Anne and her husband, were faring. There was lunch in the self-service canteen. The Queen, however, was served by the manageress, but Prince Philip and Andrew helped themselves. Andrew left his parents and sat with some of the competitors – girls. He was soon in earnest conversation with a sixteen-year-old swimmer, Nancy Garapick.

But the big event for the family was the equestrian competition in which Anne was taking part. It was a Three-Day Event – the first day, dressage; the second, steeplechase and cross-country; the third, show-jumping. For ten years Anne had devoted herself to becoming a first-class horsewoman. She had said, 'It's the one thing that the world can see I can do well that's got *nothing* whatever to do with my position, or money, or anything else.' Now here she was in Montreal, a member of the British Olympic Team, competing against the best in the world. It was not only her family and the spectators who were watching – through TV, radio and the press the world would be judging her performance. It was a daunting prospect.

She was riding Goodwill in whom she had great confidence and he had been trained to perfection. On the first day the dressage went well. On the second day she completed the steeplechase and went on to tackle the thirty-six fences of the cross-country. She was nearly halfway round when there was a mistake and she fell heavily. She lay dazed and bruised on the ground for several minutes. Then she got up, remounted and completed the course. In this class of competition, such a mistake as she had made was irreparable, but Anne is a determined woman and didn't give up. She assured her family she would be fit enough to compete on the third and final day, which she did though in some physical discomfort. She did well in the show-jumping and her final place was twenty-fourth overall.

There were no medals for the British Equestrian Team in those Games and Anne, who is fiercely competitive, was as disconsolate as anyone. But the ten years

The Queen with her three sons, Charles, Andrew and Edward, at Montreal where on 17 July 1976 she opened the Olympic Games, in which Princess Anne took part as a member of the British Equestrian Team.

On board the royal yacht *Britannia* Andrew watches one of the sailing races of the Montreal Olympic Games with his parents, the Queen and Prince Philip.

of effort had not been in vain. She had won a place in the team and she had shown skill and courage. Her family had reason to be proud of her.

For Andrew it was not all sport at Montreal. Every evening there were receptions and dances and he made the most of it all. He was now tall, towering over his mother. He was good-looking and exuberant. The schoolboy was developing into a robustly attractive young man.

He helped to give a sense of fun and lightheartedness which was needed to dispel some of the troubles at Montreal. It was a help to Pierre Trudeau for there was much at stake and being a charismatic, extrovert man himself he appreciated Andrew's attitude to life. Andrew met and was able to observe Mr Trudeau's wife, Margaret, the young woman of wayward charms who was later to revert to the pattern of life she had chosen as a girl when she joined a commune of 'beautiful people' in Morocco. However, Andrew did not observe her as closely as his brother Charles, whom she embarrassed by accusing him of ogling her bosom when they were dancing. 'Feast while ye may,' she said to him. 'If I wasn't three months pregnant there would be nothing to see!'

Andrew's acquaintance with Pierre Trudeau was fruitful. The Queen and Prince Philip had been delighted by the result of Charles spending six months in Australia at Timbertop, the outback camp of Geelong Grammar School. It had been the making of him and had also strengthened the links of the monarchy with an important member of the Commonwealth. Now a plan for Andrew to spend some time at a school in Canada was mooted and generally approved. Mr Trudeau liked Andrew and realized that his presence would have a certain political value. Canada, apart from the special problems of Quebec, has endemic difficulties in preserving its identity in the face of overwhelming influence from the United States. The Queen obviously appreciated this. Prince Philip, who may well have started the ball rolling, was enthusiastic because he wanted his sons to vary their experience and get to know the Commonwealth as young as possible. It was not exactly an accident that he also knew just the right school: Lakefield College School, about seventy miles north-east of Toronto in Ontario, which he had visited in 1969 to present medals won by boys in his own Duke of Edinburgh's Award Scheme. Lakefield had for some time been influenced by the Gordonstoun system and had operated an exchange scheme with the school for some years.

All concerned gave provisional agreement. Andrew was delighted at the prospect. Colonel Frank McEachren, who as President of the Canadian section of Prince Philip's Award Scheme was a confidant, was to organize matters in Canada. His position as senior ADC to the Lieutenant-Governor of Ontario was also a help. Back in London it would be necessary to get the approval of the Prime Minister, Mr James Callaghan, but no difficulty was expected in that quarter.

So when Andrew flew back with his mother and Edward on 26 July, he could feel fairly confident that at the beginning of the new year, 1977, he would be back in Canada. Prince Charles flew back separately to England, for it is a sensible rule that the monarch and heir do not travel in the same aircraft. Prince Philip, who is President of the International Equestrian Federation, stayed on to see the end of the Games with Anne and her husband.

Lakefield was founded a century ago to provide an education on the lines of an English public school for the boys of well-to-do families. It has acquired considerable prestige and to have been to Lakefield carries a certain social cachet. There are only 240 boys and the school has resisted expansion and the admission of girls, but they are invited along to fairly frequent dances and social evenings. Fees for a boarder are around £3,000 a year and limits the entry to families in the upper-income bracket.

Academically the school has quite a good reputation, but there is a strong emphasis on sport. The Canadians are a hardy race and they like their boys to be brought up husky. At Lakefield there is swimming, sailing and canoeing on the nearby lake. In the winter ice hockey and ski-ing are the favoured sports. There is also Canadian football, and rugby and cricket to give an English flavour.

The uniform is simple – blue trousers, a white shirt and a V-neck pullover. Discipline seems on the surface free and easy, but underneath is quite strict with punishments of early-morning runs and withdrawals of privileges. By Canadian standards creature comforts are austere, but in comparison with Gordonstoun and many English public schools more than adequate.

The school can afford to have a hand-picked staff, led by a youngish headmaster, Terence Guest, who at this time was thirty-seven and a good all-round sportsman.

Altogether it was a school well-suited to Prince Andrew.

After the excitement of the Olympic Games he had a peaceful holiday at Balmoral with the family and went back to Gordonstoun for the autumn term. With his O-levels behind him he was now a senior with the privilege of his own study. Arrangements for his six months in Canada at Lakeside were finalized and he was told he would be off at the beginning of January. Before Lakeside broke up for the Christmas holidays Mr Guest informed the boys at one of the regular Saturday morning assemblies. These were more democratic than would be likely in England – for example, complaints could be voiced and regularly at least one boy stood up and criticized the quality and quantity of the food. However, this Saturday the boys forgot to complain in the excitement that followed the announcement that Prince Andrew would be joining them in January. They were also told that during the Christmas holiday £40,000 was to be spent on a general clean-up. The dining-hall was to be painted and the kitchens were to get some new equipment. It induced a feeling that with a bit of luck the arrival of the Prince presaged an improvement in the food – and that feeling no doubt helped to ensure him a hearty welcome.

One of the boys already knew Andrew and was consequently closely questioned. He was Donald Grant, eighteen, who had been an exchange student at Gordonstoun and a room-mate of Andrew in an eighteen-bed dormitory. He was rather looking forward to meeting Andrew in a game of ice-hockey – 'the kind of hockey game that men play'. He had not forgotten the ragging he got from Andrew and other boys when he had gone confidently on to the field to play in a game of ordinary hockey and found himself penalized for just about every move he made – nobody had told him the rules were different.

Term ended at Gordonstoun and Andrew came down to London. Prince Charles was leaving the Navy before Christmas after nearly five years' service. As a parting gesture it was arranged that he should bring up his ship, HMS *Bronington*, to Tower Basin and let reporters and photographers come on board. He also invited Andrew to have a look round and photographs were taken showing Charles explaining the intricacies of the bridge to his younger brother, who looked as if it was all a huge joke.

During the family festivities there was plenty to talk about. In the New Year, 1977, the Queen was celebrating her Silver Jubilee. Apart from tours of the Commonwealth, she would be visiting many parts of Britain. But the focus of all the celebrations was to be in St Paul's Cathedral on 7 June at a service of national thanksgiving for the Queen's twenty-five years of service. Although it meant leaving Lakeside a week or so before the end of the summer term Andrew was told he would be coming back to take part in the main ceremonies and enjoy some of the fun.

On Monday, 3 January, Andrew set off for Canada with all the agreeable royal privileges of travel. He travelled in a royal car with his detective to London Airport. His luggage had been sent in another vehicle and seen through the formalities. He was travelling as Andrew Cambridge, but senior airport officials greeted him and escorted him to the special lounge. Then it was time to board the British Airways 747 for Toronto. Policemen saluted; officials saw him to the plane. In the first-class compartment a corner had been reserved so that no one was too near the Prince. The captain introduced himself. The cabin staff gave instant service throughout the flight. The plane touched down in the afternoon at Toronto Airport and as soon as the doors were opened in came Colonel McEachren, who was to be in overall charge of Andrew's stay in Canada. Andrew shook hands with the aircrew and stepped out with the Colonel. In the terminal the Lieutenant-

Sandi Jones acted as guide to Andrew at the Montreal Olympic Games and was much envied by other girls. When he went to Lakefield College School in Ontario the following year she was invited to one of the dances and had a day's ski-ing with him.

During the 1976 exercises in the Firth of Forth Prince Charles invited his brother Andrew aboard HMS *Bronington*, the 360-ton minehunter which he commanded towards the end of his five years' service with the Royal Navy.

Governor, Mrs Pauline McGibbon, was waiting with her husband and an aide-de-camp to greet him.

The word had gone round the airport that Andrew had arrived and by the time he got into the official limousine with the Colonel a group of fifty spectators, mainly girls, had gathered. Andrew was not going to let an opportunity like that pass. He wound down the car window and asked some of the girls, 'What's the weather like?' 'Cold, real cold!' came the answer. It was minus five degrees Centigrade. 'Does it get any colder?' he asked. 'Much, much colder,' he was told. 'Well, I'll have to get some warmer clothes,' he said with a laugh. Then he drove off to stay the night with the McEachren's in their very handsome home.

But Andrew's harmless enough remarks were reported and inspired a spiteful little article by a woman columnist, Claire Hay, in the *Toronto Sun*. Prince Andrew, she wrote, should have known better than to ask if it was cold in Canada at that time of the year. 'Yes, it is,' she went on angrily. 'It is also, despite what the Brits would like to tell each other, civilised!' She ended by commenting that presumably the royal family had thought, 'Wouldn't it be charming to send H.R.H. out to the colonies!' The woman columnist had probably written in that style just to be different, for Andrew had a very good press reception and photographs of his arrival were widely carried with agreeable comments. However, she got the publicity she had no doubt wanted – hundreds of telephone protests.

The next morning Andrew was received officially at the Lieutenant-General's office in the Ontario Legislature buildings and gave a brief press conference. He was given a very easy time by the reporters for editors had been asked to co-operate by treating him as a welcome guest who at sixteen was still only a schoolboy. When all the formalities were over Andrew was given lunch and then Colonel McEachren drove him to Lakefield to meet Terry Guest and his wife, Sue. The next day term started.

Canadians may not be used to dealing daily with a prince, but they like to get things right, so after discussion with various officials Mr Guest laid down the following rules of protocol. 'The boys would call him Andrew,' he instructed. 'The staff would address him as Prince Andrew, the governors would call him Sir, and the chairman of the governors alone would give him the full Your Royal Highness.' These were sensible instructions – except for the boys. After the first day Andrew became 'Andy'. Before he left it was 'Randy Andy'.

There was another more important problem – security. The Royal Canadian Mounted Police, which is now the equivalent of Scotland Yard and more in Canada, were responsible. They provided a personal detective, Corporal John Ellis. They also had to keep surveillance over the school for there were dangers of kidnapping for money, as well as from extremists in Quebec.

Andrew had no problem settling in. The other boys liked him and he liked them. Within a few weeks he said:

The school is quite excellent and so are all the facilities that it offers. But it's not just that – the boys here are terrific, really great. They are different from the chaps in England because they have a different outlook from a different country. On top of all that everyone in Canada is incredibly friendly. You can say that life out here is very good indeed.

Andrew's remarks about life in Canada echoed those made by Charles when he spent some months at Timbertop in Australia. There does not seem to be any reason to doubt the sincerity of either. In both cases they were reacting with surprised pleasure to an environment that was more free and dynamic than that in Britain. Soon after he arrived he met the boy who, under the exchange scheme, would replace him at Gordonstoun. This gave him a chance to let himself go and issue a dire warning: 'The beds are as hard as iron. It's straw mattresses and bread and water. It's just like a prison.'

He soon showed himself to be quite a good skier. He had had some experience in Scotland, but probably Prince Philip had taken him a few times to Germany during the Christmas holidays on ski-ing holidays with his young cousins. He had done the same with Charles and Anne and publicity had made the trips somewhat disastrous. But with Andrew he seems to have been more successful in preserving privacy.

Andrew was soon learning to play ice-hockey, but found he had a long way to go in a game which the other boys had been brought up with since they could walk. He went with the school team for an away match at Pittsburgh in the United States and soon found himself surrounded by half-a-dozen girls – most of them the friends of the Pittsburgh team. 'I think some of the Pittsburgh guys were getting a bit worried,' said Al Pace, one of the Lakefield star players. 'He really attracts the ladies!'

One of the girls went to tell her mother that there was a prince in the crowd. But mother, unimpressed, suggested that it was one of those Arab princes who are fairly thick on the ground in America these days. 'Naw mom,' said the daughter. 'He's the son of the Queen of England!' Mom was then suitably impressed.

The first dance of the term was to be given on Saturday, 22 January. The girls invited generally came from schools in Lakefield or nearby towns such as Peterborough or Coburg and a few who made the journey from Toronto. Andrew was told there would be more than enough to go round. But then he remembered the pretty girl, Sandi Jones, who had been his guide the previous year at the Olympic yachting events at Kingston. He found out that she lived at Kingston with her parents, Colonel Campbell Jones, a retired Canadian army officer, and his wife, Eileen, who was British-born. So he telephoned her and asked if she could come to the dance. She was, as she said, 'flabbergasted', but recovered quickly the poise of a well brought up Canadian girl and said that she would be delighted to come if she got a written invitation from the headmaster's wife. All was arranged according to protocol and Sandi was to spend the night with Mr and Mrs Guest.

Sandi looked very pretty indeed at the dance in a silver-coloured jacket and red skirt. But she did not make friends among the other girls as Andrew danced with her most of the evening. 'It was unfair,' said one of the disgruntled. 'A lot of us would have loved to have asked him to dance.' However, the doughnuts were munched, the fruit-juice drunk and Sandi survived the death-wishing glances of the other daughters of Canada.

On Sunday Andrew took Sandi on a long cross-country ski and the detective agreed to let him go without him providing he took a walkie-talkie. In the evening he drove over to Coburg with her and before she got in the train gave her a hug and a kiss. Sandi, back at Kingston Vocational Collegiate Institute next morning, didn't know whether she was on her head or her heels. 'The two most exciting days of my life,' summed up her feelings.

It was a wonderful winter for Andrew. There was downhill ski-ing from Cedar Mountain in the sparkling, crisp air. There was ice-hockey, played at a breath-taking pace. There were many new friends telling him about their lives in Canada. There was also a certain amount of study.

The Easter holidays were well-planned. He was to spend a few days ski-ing with Pierre Trudeau and his wife and their children Sacha, Justin and Michel; a few days in Toronto to see the sights; and then a stay with a schoolfriend, Peter Lorriman, whose father, a rich industrialist, had an estate, Brolor Farm, near Orangeville in Ontario.

Andrew, who had had his seventeenth birthday in February, had kept in touch with Sandi Jones. Conveniently it happened that she had an aunt living in Toronto with whom she could stay when he was visiting the city. So Sandi helped him to enjoy the sights. They went to a jazz concert given by a Scot, Jim Galloway. They had dinner at the new Harbour Castle Hotel which is the smartest and most expensive in the city with a spectacular view of the Harbour.

Andrew had said that he likes playing roles in life and he certainly was taking on a Canadian part now. He had bought some Canadian clothes and walked around in a loosely-cut suit, with a wide-check shirt and a boot-lace tie, all crowned with a city version of a wide-brimmed cowboy hat.

At Brolor Farm Andrew was able to take part in one of the great Canadian traditions. There were many sugar maples on the estate and in March they are

In January 1977 Andrew went to Canada to spend six months at Lakefield College School in Ontario. Here he is clearing a gate on the slalom run while practising with the ski team.

Andrew tasting maple syrup on the Lorrimans' farm in Ontario.

Playing hockey at Lakefield College School. As it is a traditional game at Gordonstoun he is an experienced player.

tapped by boring holes and collecting the juice which is then evaporated into the incomparable maple syrup. Andrew did his best to help. Mrs Lorriman, who has six sons, enjoyed having Andrew to stay and said that he fitted in 'just like one of the family'.

One way and another it could be said that, even at this halfway stage of his stay in Canada, Andrew was doing a power of good to Anglo-Canadian relations – no mean achievement for a young man just turned seventeen.

Back at Lakefield for the summer term Andrew was able to show his skill at rugby and cricket. The winter in Canada is so long and the snow lies so deep that rugby is played in the summer and early autumn only. As for cricket, the first job for the boys, as Terry Guest said, is to clear the snow from the pitch. When the rugby team turned out, with Andrew playing a useful full back, there always seemed to be a row of pretty girls watching from the touchline, some of them wearing T-shirts bearing the slogan 'Andy for King'. With the good coaching and experience he had had he was an asset to the cricket team.

The school encourages amateur dramatics and Andrew appeared in two productions – in both cases as an old man. In the first he was an unfortunate who was slowly poisoned, but in the next he played Mr Brownlow in *Oliver*, wearing a top hat and long whiskers. Mr Brownlow is the benevolent old gentleman who befriends Oliver and later discovers he is his grandson. Girls from a nearby school played the female parts and Gillian Wilson, aged sixteen, played Nancy. When Mr Brownlow discovered Nancy lying in the gutter and got down on one knee to feel her pulse, Gillian's heart was pulsing madly although poor Nancy was meant to be dead.

Andrew carried out his duties as a senior boy, supervising and taking prep. By all accounts he seemed to have become in personality a more rounded young man. He was still breezy and tough, but he smiled more often and was losing some of the needless aggression that had made him at times an awkward character at school in Britain. So far as his studies were concerned Andrew probably realized that they were suffering from the change of curriculum and methods, but he was benefiting in many other ways.

April and May swept by and it was time for him to fly back to England for the Silver Jubilee celebrations. It was goodbye to Lakefield but not to Canada and his friends. He was to come back later in the year to make a tour of western Canada and then Terry Guest was taking him and four of his schoolfriends on an adventure canoeing trip down the Coppermine River which involved going well into the Arctic Circle.

Andrew flew back to London on 3 June, and when he landed at Heathrow his appearance showed something of the change in him. He had gone out

Down the steps of St Paul's Cathedral the Queen Mother is escorted by her three grandsons, Charles, Andrew and Edward after the memorable Service of Thanksgiving to mark the Queen's Silver Jubilee on 7 June 1977.

Andrew and Edward share in the great upsurge of national rejoicing as they drive away from the Service of Thanksgiving in St Paul's.

soberly dressed in a suit; he came back in an open-neck checked shirt, no jacket, casual trousers and was carrying his own case. He also looked happy and very handsome.

He had much to tell his family, and there was much to tell him. It was good to see Anne, who was expecting a baby in November, and she and Mark were able to tell him about the renovations at Gatcombe Park, the estate in the Cotswolds the Queen had given them. Edward was to start at Gordonstoun in the autumn. Charles had been touring Commonwealth countries in Africa and was now busy as chairman of the Silver Jubilee Appeal raising money for youth projects. And there was another subject the brothers could now discuss on a more equal basis – girlfriends. Andrew, only seventeen and over eleven years younger than Charles, was making a good start and it was clear he was not going to be left far behind in that race.

It was good that Andrew was able to experience the great upsurge of national emotion that marked the Silver Jubilee of his mother, the Queen. The intensity of the feelings, a mixture of affection for the person and pride in the nationhood which she symbolized, caught Fleet Street completely off balance. Its editors had, for the most part, projected for years with a fierce masochistic pleasure a Britain that was almost ungovernable, riven by strikes and bloody-mindedness and uncaring of its traditions and institutions.

Perhaps the most telling comment was by the people responsible for the flower-beds in front of Buckingham Palace. In spite of massive television and radio coverage which might have kept them at home, nearly a million people, as *The Times* reported, went out to greet the Queen on Silver Jubilee Day in London. Hundreds of thousands stood before the Palace in the evening to call for the Queen to appear on the balcony – which she did many times with the family. The next day the gardeners reported that scarcely a plant had been trodden on – so disciplined had been the crowd.

The day had begun with a service of thanksgiving in St Paul's Cathedral. Andrew with Edward was seated by the Queen Mother under the great dome and saw and heard the ritual splendour of the established Church of England as it celebrated the occasion before God to a congregation that comprised the establishment of the nation and the representatives of the Commonwealth and the world. It was followed by a supremely successful walk-about by the Queen and Prince Philip on their way to Guildhall for the feast given by the Lord Mayor and Corporation of London.

There were other less solemn, but heart-warming events. In Windsor Great Park the Queen lit the first bonfire which gave the signal to start a chain of others which burst into flame the length and breadth of the island from Land's End to John O'Groats. There was the spectacular firework display on the Thames

The balcony scene on Silver Jubilee Day when a million people made their way to Buckingham Palace to greet the Queen and her family. Lord Mountbatten was by the Queen's side to share this day of national rejoicing with Prince Philip, the three sons, Charles, Andrew and Edward, and Princess Anne with Captain Mark Phillips.

Prince Andrew helped to give a sense of fun during the great gathering of young people at the new University of Ulster in Coleraine when the Queen visited the province during her Silver Jubilee tours in 1977.

Andrew and Charles share a joke at the Braemar Games which they were visiting as usual while on holiday at Balmoral.

followed by a procession of illuminated craft that stretched for miles either side of London. There were the children's parties in many humble, ordinary streets with the adults relaxing after the event in the local public houses.

Andrew, like the rest of the family, was involved in all this celebration either as a direct spectator or through television. These days gave him as never before an insight into the quality of his mother and the meaning of monarchy to the British.

Marvellous as all this was for a young man, Andrew flew back to Canada with the anticipation of a wonderful trip ahead. This time he made sure that he had his painting equipment with him, for he wanted to record some of his experiences. His father painted, so did Charles and he himself enjoyed trying to put on a canvas not so much what he saw as the patterns the scenes evoked in him. Unlike his father and brother he was drawn to abstract painting.

First he flew to Toronto and stayed with Colonel McEachren, who had invited some of the Lakefield boys. There were a lot of fun and games, visits to neighbours, sailing and before the end a dance to which it was no surprise that Sandi Jones was invited. After the round of parties, Andrew was to visit Alberta and British Columbia in the west.

The west is about two thousand miles from Toronto and even at the speed of a jet the journey impresses on the first-time traveller something of the dimension of the country, but it does nothing to prepare the mind of the European for the experience of the Rocky Mountains as you approach them by road after landing at Calgary. No one could fail to be struck with wonder as from Banff onwards spectacle after spectacle surfeits the senses.

The chain of national parks stretches for hundreds of miles – Jasper, Banff, Glacier, Mount Revelstoke, Kootenay, Waterton. The area is so huge that even in the tourist season when Andrew was there deep solitude can be found not far from the main roads. There are vast lakes enclosed by great mountains, alpine meadows covered in wild flowers, vertiginous gorges and canyons. But it was the wildlife, now fortunately protected, that brought the final satisfaction to Andrew – as it does to most visitors. As a privileged guest everyone wanted him to experience to the full what the area has to offer. In Waterton National Park he was able to visit a naturalist's paradise. It is the home of grizzly bears, black bears, mule deer, beavers, cougars, marmots, foxes and weasels. Overhead are innumerable song-birds while above them soar hawks, falcons and eagles. Before he left the parks Andrew was inducted into the Canadian Branch of the World Wildlife Fund which was a way of ensuring that he continued to take an interest in its work of preservation.

Before touring the National Parks Andrew had a day or two in Calgary, a

When his stay at Lakefield was over Andrew was given a splendid holiday in Canada.
Here he is at the Calgary Stampede, suitably dressed for the occasion.

splendid, dynamic city made rich by the surrounding oilfields. The Calgary Stampede, held in the first two weeks of July, is billed as 'The Greatest Dad-burned Show on Earth', with $150,000 in prize money for the rodeo competitors and daily chuckwagon (pioneer wagons) races between four wagons, twenty men and thirty-two thoroughbreds. There are stage shows, livestock exhibitions, dancing in the streets, cowboys and Indians. It is great fun and, what is more, Andrew had a pretty girl, Gillian Newman, to describe the technicalities of rodeo. He left another girl starry-eyed behind him. 'He's Prince Charming,' she said, sighing.

In British Columbia Andrew found himself taking part – not fortuitously – in the 110th anniversary of the birth of the Dominion of Canada in 1867. A 110th anniversary might not seem to be very significant, but Mr Trudeau and his Government were doing their utmost to stress the unity of the nation and decided to spend several million dollars on the festivities. In the federal capital, Ottawa, there was a great gathering on Parliament Hill ending in a lavish firework display. But events were organized in all the provinces, including British Columbia, especially in its capital, Vancouver. Andrew was welcome there as a son of the Queen, a potent symbol of the unity of Canada and also of its status as a senior member of the Commonwealth. He was also welcome for himself for he had won a reputation as a lively, informal and tough young man at Lakefield.

He saw the sights, attended receptions and informal parties, thoroughly enjoyed himself and left behind him a sense of shared pleasure. At seventeen Andrew was doing a diplomat's job – and doing it well. But it was not as if he was going through the ritual in the dark. He knew very well what it was all about, partly by his native intelligence and partly by the expert advice he was receiving.

Apart from this semi-official role it was a wonderful experience for Andrew. He was shown Vancouver Bay, one of the sights of the world, with the great seaport of over a million people lying round its shores and framed by a ring of spectacular mountains. Everywhere Andrew was seeing scenery on a scale that widened the concept of life for a young man whose vision had previously been limited to western Europe. In the 1,000 acres of Stanley Park with its 100,000 trees, he visited the beaches, the zoo and the remarkable aquarium with its 8,300 animals, including a killer shark which was put through its repertoire by the trainer, Klaus Michaelis. Andrew met young people – including more than enough pretty girls – went out to restaurants and discos. He was always smiling and never seemed tired.

Andrew then flew to Edmonton, the capital of Alberta and the take-off point for the north. He joined up with Terry Guest, who had with him another master and four boys from Lakefield. All was set for the final phase of Andrew's Canadian tour – the two-week journey of three hundred miles by canoe down the Coppermine River to the Arctic.

Such is the cussedness of life that English people read and talk more about the tundra, permafrost, vast spaces and potential wealth of Siberia than they do about the Northwest Territories of Canada. But it is much the same story – the north of Canada is the Siberia of the American continent and it has been opened up to a large extent by people of British stock and there are no slave camps.

Even today, when air-travel and technology have taken away some of the hardships of life in the area and when tourism is possible in the few summer months, the north retains an almost mystical influence on Canadians – it has always been the ultimate challenge luring men to its vast desolation with promises of gold or the limitless wealth of oil and minerals. Andrew had been in Canada long enough to feel this. Some of the families of the boys who enjoyed the privileges of Lakefield had wrested their prosperity not in the offices of Toronto but in opening up the north.

To go north from Edmonton you fly by scheduled aircraft about eight hundred miles to Yellowknife on the Great Slave Lake. This town of ten thousand is the capital of the Northwest Territories and now has office blocks, hotels, restaurants and all the amenities of a modern city. It is the outpost headquarters of many lumber and mining companies and there are sizeable gold mines in the area. In the summer months there are many comfortable fishing lodges open now on the lakes and people come from distant cities of Canada and the United States to recharge their batteries in the solitude of empty spaces.

Andrew's party still had another three hundred miles to go northwards. There are many charter air companies in Yellowknife servicing the lumber and mining settlements and ferrying the tourists in the short summer. Once you take off from Yellowknife it is desolate country. The tree belt, which brings so much wealth to the country, thins and then there is little to see but small birch and stunted willow. What look like emerald green fields from the air are bottomless morasses. This was the land of the trapper operating from the Hudson's Bay Company Forts that were the only human settlements apart from scattered Indian camps. Andrew's party landed at a camp on the Coppermine and sorted out its equipment. There are placid lakes and rivers in the north where canoeing is a relatively easy-going pastime. The Coppermine is not one of these. It may not be as dangerous as the South Redstone, the South Nahanni or the Dubawnt, but it is a challenge even for the experienced canoeist. The course is tortuous, the current treacherous, the rapids and falls hazardous. Terry Guest and his colleague are experienced Arctic canoeists, but the Coppermine is a test even for them.

The party was travelling in two-man canoes, taking all their food and camping equipment. The plague of black flies that make life miserable at this time of the year was past its worst, but protective ointment, frequently renewed, takes away the worst discomfort. There were about three hundred miles to reach the mouth of the Coppermine where there is a settlement of the same name. About halfway they would cross the Arctic Circle.

It was a demanding journey, even for fit young men, and at the end of the day the work of pitching camp, lighting a fire and cooking left everyone with just about enough energy to creep into a sleeping-bag. Every day had its mishaps, such as a canoe capsizing and leaving the crew swimming in very cold water indeed.

As you travel north there is little scenery – just an increase of desolation. There is little game in the area, but now and again you might catch a sight of bear, deer or wolves. At this time of the year, however the air is filled with birds – geese, duck, sandpipers, and eagles and falcons follow them as predators. A light fog tends to come down in the late afternoon and shrouds the mire and coarse vegetation. It is time to finish the day – although in summer there is little dark at night in these latitudes. At first the weather is generally muggy and overcast, but as you go north there are clear skies and a tonic quality in the air.

Andrew, who was travelling in the same canoe as Terry Guest, paddled on day after day. Even though he was travelling in some comfort and with experts to guide him, he was getting the feel of the north. It is a land that can strike terror even in the most doughty heart. It is the size of it and the emptiness of it – and just about every aspect seems hostile to human life. It is as if man had no place there and would always be an intruder. Sometimes it looks like the chaos before the world was created. The north has driven many a man mad, in spite of all the help modern technology has brought to the area.

However, the last rapids and falls were overcome by the Lakefield party and they passed the swamps, covered in wildfowl, at the mouth of the river. After the loneliness of the journey Coppermine itself seems quite a lively, cheerful little place and boasts a hotel, the Igloo Inn, which is open all the year round. The population is largely Eskimo who live by hunting whale, caribou (the North American reindeer), polar bear and white fox. They are the Copper Eskimos, the last to come into contact with the white man. They have preserved some of their elaborate culture, including dancing costumes of intricate design and many colours. The name of Coppermine is misleading. There are no copper mines either on the river or round the settlement. The river was named by an eighteenth-century traveller, Samuel Hearne, who thought there was copper on its banks – who knows, he may one day be proved right!

Andrew and the party rested for a day or two. All had reason to feel pleased with themselves. It had been a success and no one had come to more harm than

This was the tough side of Andrew's Canadian holiday. Here he is with Terry Guest, the headmaster of Lakefield, who took him and a small group of boys on an adventurous 200-mile canoeing trip down the Coppermine River to the Arctic Ocean.

The Canadian style: Andrew at the end of his two terms at Lakefield College School in Ontario.

blistered hands and a few grazes. Andrew saw the Arctic Ocean which comes in here through the Coronation Gulf. It laps the shore peacefully enough at this time of the year, so peacefully that it has a sinister air.

The party flew back to Edmonton and ordinary life began again. Andrew was greeted by the Lieutenant-Governor of Alberta, Ralph Steinhauer, and by this time everyone was beginning to think that Andrew was part of the Canadian scene. But on 30 July he caught a plane back to London. His great Canadian experience was over.

The six months his brother Charles had spent in Australia when he was seventeen had changed his entire outlook on life. He went out there still shy, diffident and inward-looking. He came back self-confident and able to face life with a smile. As he said, it was 'the most wonderful experience I've ever had, I think'.

Andrew had gone to Canada a young man, full of self-confidence and bounce. He had for years expressed himself with a jaunty, at times annoying aggressive-ness. Canada had taught him that there were other young men, self-confident and physically tough, who were nevertheless modest and cared about other people. The lesson was not lost on Andrew. Because of who he was, he had been given the tour of a lifetime. He had seen more of Canada than many Canadians ever see. He had visited their great cities and enjoyed their comfort and sophistication. But he had also seen, in the east and the north, a country with a dimension that dwarfed his previous experiences. He had witnessed some of the daunting challenges men face in developing such a country. They were more than enough to take the bounce out of a young man who had been as protected as Andrew.

If Canada had given him much, it must be said that in return Andrew had done his best. He was the sort of vigorous, healthy young man who goes down well with the Canadians, but he had shown that there was a bit more to him than that, even at his age. He had listened, he had learned and he had charmed important men and women with his courtesy and understanding. He was acquiring a princely style of his own. It was not that of his father, nor even that of his elder brother. He could communicate his own sense of pleasure in life, but he was learning to control his ebullience with a certain shrewdness that came from a growing intelligence.

Canada was going through a difficult time. It has had its ups and downs economically in the past, but they were not much more than growing pains. Its real problems are its unity and identity. The separatist movement in Quebec is a threat to its unity. The influence of the United States both culturally and finan-cially is a threat to its identity.

The presence of Andrew and his personality had strengthened, if only a little, Canadian consciousness of its place as a growing influence in the Commonwealth, of which the British monarchy is the symbol of unity.

On a lighter, but still for a young man important, note, Andrew had clearly been much taken by Sandi Jones. An affectionate relationship plays its part in the development of character. Andrew is an attractive young man and is also a prince, so that for Sandi his charms must have been flattering, if not overwhelming.

One way and another, when Andrew landed at London Airport, he could feel Canada had been very good for him indeed.

7

Jumping for Joy

Andrew spent the week-end with his parents at Windsor. The Queen, accompanied by Prince Philip, was still busy with Jubilee visits to the provinces, but was buoyed up by the remarkable warmth of her reception everywhere. Instead of tiring her, she was drawing strength from the celebrations and a renewed sense of purpose as she realized, with a certain surprise (for she is a modest person), how deep was the affection and loyalty of the nation.

The following week Andrew went to Cowes with his father, who had a few days to spare before he joined the Queen in the royal yacht which was being used as a headquarters for the tour of the west country. Andrew, wearing a T-shirt carrying the name Lakefield, was sailing in the Flying Fifteen class aboard *Crescendo* which was owned and skippered by Mr John Terry. They were doing quite well in a competition on the second day, but broke a rudder pin and by the time it was repaired were out of the race. The old hands at Cowes were glad to see Andrew sailing in the Flying Fifteen class, for his father had as a younger man owned *Coweslip* of the same class and raced it successfully for many seasons.

When Cowes week was over, Andrew and Edward joined their parents on the royal yacht for the last and most difficult of the Jubilee tours – Ulster. Since 1969 a considerable garrison of British troops has been vainly trying to stamp out the violence and bloodshed which marks yet another phase in the struggle between the Protestant majority, which wishes to remain part of Britain, and the Catholic minority, which wants union with the Republic of Ireland. It is an unhappy and dangerous province and the gunmen and bombers of the IRA have shown in murderous forays that they could kill in England as mercilessly as in Ulster. There were many who thought that the risk to the Queen and her family was too great to justify the visit. But the fact that she had abandoned the tour would have been a moral and psychological victory for the IRA. The security men said that as far as was humanly possible they could guarantee her safety if their very stringent precautions were observed. So the Queen decided to go on with the visit. She is not foolhardy, but comes of a family that has never lacked personal courage.

The *Britannia*, closely guarded against limpet bombs, was used as the royal headquarters. The visits ashore had to be circumscribed and the number of people who saw the royal party strictly limited. One of the final engagements was the opening by the Queen of the new university at Coleraine in North Antrim near the north coast. Over 1,800 young people, representing all aspects of youth activity, had been invited to a reception following the opening ceremony. Prince Andrew flew in by helicopter from the royal yacht and by the force of his personality helped to take some of the tension out of the day and create an atmosphere of fun and laughter.

When the *Britannia* sailed safely away at the end of the visit Andrew had experienced another chapter in anti-terrorist measures which had begun when he was a small boy at preparatory school. They leave their mark.

The family went to Balmoral for the usual holiday. It had been an eventful year and everybody had plenty to talk about. Anne was heavily pregnant. She was determined to have her baby on 14 November, the fourth anniversary of her wedding-day and Charles's birthday. It seems the Queen and her family think mid-November is an auspicious time for them, which is understandable enough as she married Prince Philip on 20 November. When Charles does get married it would not be surprising if he chose a date around then – and the same might go for Andrew.

Then it was back to Gordonstoun, with Edward in tow as the new boy. After term had settled down Andrew had talks with his masters about his studies. He had taken six good O-levels the previous year and there had been talk of him taking A-levels in 1978. Inevitably, however, the months in Canada had disturbed the rhythm of his progress. It seemed best for him to wait until 1979 and make sure of good results. Charles had taken two A-levels with a 'C' in French and a 'B' in History, but he had suffered many interruptions because of his position as heir to the throne. Charles had had to work hard to get his A-levels, but he had wanted them badly as he felt he could go to Trinity at Cambridge with a reasonably clear conscience. At Gordonstoun the masters thought that if Andrew waited until 1979 he could take three A-levels – English, History and Economics and Political Sciences – which would fit him for a place in one of the more academically tough colleges, either at Oxford or Cambridge. At this time it seems to have been taken for granted that Andrew would go on to university before a spell in the services, thus following the pattern of his elder brother.

It was not all work, however. There was rugby and hockey. There were the girls – 120 of them now among the 450 pupils. In the old days at royal courts there would have been maids-of-honour or ladies-in-waiting to provide company for the young princes, but Gordonstoun was providing an even wider choice. This term a friendship developed with Kirsty Richmond, then seventeen, who had been at the school nearly as long as Andrew. She was an attractive, well-built girl, daughter of Mrs Valerie Richmond, a widow who was a school nurse living in the Suffolk village of Great Barton, near Bury-St-Edmunds. She had made sacrifices to send her daughter to Gordonstoun, but it had been worthwhile for she was turning out well and taking her A-levels in 1978. She had been part of Andrew's set for some time, but this autumn they spent more time together. Later in the term he asked his mother if Kirsty could be invited to spend a few days at Sandringham during the Christmas holidays and in due time the formal invitation arrived.

Before Andrew had gone to Balmoral he had sorted out some canvases he had painted in Canada for an exhibition in Windsor Castle to be held in October as part of the local festival. Charles, who had been painting for some years, was also showing some water-colours, an art which he found 'very difficult, but most rewarding'. Their father, Prince Philip, had already had a small exhibition of his own work shown at the Royal Academy.

The art critic of the *Sunday Telegraph*, Michael Shepherd, went along to see the Windsor exhibition, 'Royal Performance'. He praised Charles's work for its sensitivity and sense of colour and then went on: 'More surprising, though less skilled as yet, Prince Andrew, in one of his Canadian landscape paintings ... shows an adventurous sense of abstraction and composition beyond the usual admirable amateurism of royal performances.' A judgment which must have pleased.

Like any other school Gordonstoun has its share of scandals, but normally they remain private. This term, however, one became public, probably because it involved Constantine Niarchos, fifteen, the son of Mr Stavros Niarchos, the immensely rich Greek shipowner. The boy, who, it is said, will inherit £40 million when he is twenty-one, was expelled with four other boys and a girl for smoking cannabis. 'Pot' has been a problem for years in some of the most prestigious schools and expulsion had not always followed the offence. But the Gordonstoun board of governors, whose chairman is Lord Leven, backed the headmaster's decision. It was a blow to the prestige of the Niarchos family. But its prestige was maintained in another way for Constantine was picked up by a private Niarchos jet from the RAF base at Lossiemouth, not far from the school.

Andrew attended a seminar on the Common Market at the school and asked lots of questions, but he forgot Brussels and the Common Agricultural Policy soon after when he was told that Anne had had her baby, a boy. She had not quite made 14 November, for the baby arrived the next day, the fifteenth. When term ended in December Andrew and Edward flew down to London and were able to inspect their first nephew. He was christened on the twenty-second in the music room at Buckingham Palace – as they had been. He was given the names Peter Mark Andrew. Understandably it was that third name that pleased – Andrew.

Having done his Christmas shopping Andrew enjoyed himself in London for a few days. He went to late-night discos with friends and one evening arrived at the fashionable Annabel's in an open-necked shirt only to find that the management insisted on a tie even in these informal days. One was found for him quickly enough – even Annabel's doesn't turn away a royal prince – and he had a splendid evening with his party, dancing most of the time with an attractive girl, Julia Guinness, who was eighteen. 'He is a bit of a flirt,' she had commented later, 'but the most charming person you could hope to meet.'

Christmas was a time for exchanging news, as with most families. Anne's husband, Mark Phillips, was giving up the army. His promotion chances were almost nil as he was debarred from a posting to Northern Ireland. So he was to do a year's training at the Royal Agricultural College at Cirencester and then farm the Gatcombe Park estate. Charles had had a good tour of Australia in the autumn. But above all the family could look back with unalloyed pleasure to the success the Queen had enjoyed during her Silver Jubilee. It had surpassed all expectations – her children had reason to be specially proud of their mother when the toasts were drunk at the end of Christmas dinner.

In the New Year Kirsty Richmond arrived at Sandringham for her stay. However easy Andrew and his family made her path, it must have been quite an ordeal for a girl brought up in quite modest circumstances. To the royal family Sandringham may be just the country home in Norfolk, but to most people it has the dimensions and grandeur of a palace. To Kirsty, however, probably the most intimidating aspect was the number of servants. It is possible if you have a strong character, as Kirsty has, to cope with grand people, but their servants have a way, perhaps almost unconscious, of cutting you down to size. Kirsty is, however, a girl brought up in the country and much of the day at Sandringham is spent outdoors. There are horses to ride, guns to use or follow, long walks. It is certain that Kirsty was a welcome guest not only to Andrew – she is a charming person and the Queen and Prince Philip were quick to recognize this.

Holidays over, it was back to Gordonstoun. Apart from work and games Andrew was celebrating a specially important birthday on 19 February. He would be eighteen that year, 1978, and come of age. He would also from that day be entitled to £20,000 per annum from the Civil List grants made by Parliament to the royal family. It was only natural that he was not only aware of this, but pleased at the prospect. The royal family is very money-conscious and Andrew is no exception. He knew, as he somewhat ruefully remarked, that he would not be seeing much of the money for some time. The Queen had told him that she would let him have £600 a year to spend and that the rest would be invested. She later informed Parliament of her decision, making the point that Andrew was not as yet undertaking any royal duties. This was an important point, for the Queen and her advisers have in her reign gradually, but significantly, modified the concept of the grants made under the Civil List. In a more grandiose past the allowances made to the royal family, with the exception of the monarch who has constitutional duties to perform, had tended to be considered as grants-in-aid to support a reasonably grand life-style to give dignity to the Crown and the nation. In this reign, however, a leaf has been taken out of modern business practice, and the grants from the Civil List have been presented more as expense accounts than as allowances. It has been a clever move. It disarms criticism that large sums of public money are being paid out to hangers-on. It reinforces the argument that those receiving grants earn them by their public duties. It is also a help with the tax-man for only the Queen is exempt from his demands.

Though Andrew might have thought that £600 a year was not much out of £20,000, he lived free and enjoyed immense privileges already such as free travel. The balance, being invested, would provide a useful nest-egg later on. In addition he knew that, under provisions made by Parliament many years ago when the Queen came to the throne, when he got married his Civil List grant would be increased to £50,000 per annum. Under the same provisions his younger brother, Edward, would be treated exactly the same. However, Andrew can also count on the generosity of his mother in the future. The size of the Queen's private fortune is a closely guarded secret, but it is known she is a very wealthy woman. Conservative estimates place it around £20–£30 million. It has been amassed in the comparatively short time of just over a century and owes its origin to the financial prudence of Prince Albert, the husband of Queen Victoria.

Thanks to Albert, the Balmoral estate was bought by Victoria as a personal possession. Thanks to him again, the Sandringham estate was bought, primarily for the then Prince of Wales, later Edward VII. Queen Elizabeth in 1978 bought 6,700 acres of grouse-shooting moors near Balmoral for £750,000. She has also been very generous to her daughter, Anne. The Gatcombe Park estate in the Cotswolds covers 1,200 acres and is a fine home and a valuable farming property.

So it is possible that Andrew, and in time his younger brother, Edward, may also be given estates. But that is a personal matter for the Queen. It might be optimistic to think that because one estate has been given others will follow. For example, Princess Margaret, the Queen's only sister, has no country home or estate.

While it might be an exaggeration to use the adjective parsimonious, Andrew was certainly brought up with a careful attitude towards money. The Queen likes to keep up her position and in her day has spent largely on her racing stable, but she is cautious about money, as she is about most things. Prince Philip, who spent an almost penniless youth dependent on rich relatives, cannot bear waste. His financial insecurity before his marriage made him determined that his children

His Royal Highness Prince Andrew on his eighteenth birthday, 19 February 1978.

should be brought up to understand the value of money and never forget it. Charles was kept so short of pocket-money at school that most of the time he was broke which led to the unjust accusation that he had himself sold his essay-books which ended up being published by a German magazine. Andrew planned his expenditure more carefully, but was often short.

On his mother's side Andrew's family has a varied record about money. King George VI was economical, but his brother, Edward VIII, lavished expensive jewellery on Wallis Simpson when he was Prince of Wales and sadly depleted the finances of the Duchy of Cornwall for a generation. George V believed the monarchy should live in great style, but was careful. His father, Edward VII, was a great spender of money both as Prince of Wales and King. But he was clever and made sure that the Jewish financiers who surrounded him were in a position to make him large fortunes on the Stock Exchange. His closest adviser in these matters was the brilliant Sir Ernest Cassel, who had come over from Germany as a young man and made a vast fortune here. His granddaughter, Edwina, was his heiress and brought great wealth when she married Lord Louis (later Earl) Mountbatten.

Andrew's eighteenth birthday attracted the interest of the press and numerous articles were published. Audrey Whiting wrote in the *Sunday Mirror*: 'The generally-held opinion in court circles is that he is by far the most outstanding boy in the royal trio. . . . All the drive and personal dynamism of his father combined with the Queen's sense of diplomacy. . . . More self-confident and self-assured than Charles at thirty'. Even the magic word 'charisma' was used.

In any event, this spring of 1978 the two brothers were going to share the excitement and hazards of parachuting training. Charles had already had some experience as part of his RAF training in 1971. He had parachuted into the Channel to gain experience of pilot ejection procedure. Since then, however, he had been appointed Colonel-in-Chief of the Parachute Regiment and felt he could not share the very special elan of the unit until he had won his parachute badge to add to his wings. Andrew now got into the act and got his parents' permission to take the parachute course during his Easter holidays at the same time as his brother.

However meticulous the training procedures that have gradually been evolved, to earn a parachute badge is still a mark of courage in a young man and since their use in the war parachute regiments of all nations have rightly enjoyed a special prestige. They are élite troops. So the decision of Charles and Andrew to qualify does give a measure of their spirit. It is not really surprising that the Queen and Prince Philip had no objections to their first and second sons going on the course – it was in the family tradition. In 1879 the Duke of Clarence, the eldest son of the

Charles and Andrew shared a parachute jumping course at Brize Norton, in Oxfordshire, in April 1978. Here they are laughing through a ground training session.

Andrew fastening his straps during a further stage of ground training in his parachute course.

then Prince of Wales (later Edward VII), and his brother George (later George V), were sent off as boys on a three-year cruise in HMS *Bacchante* when they had passed out of the Royal Naval College. Disraeli, then Prime Minister, discussed the matter with the First Lord of the Admiralty and wrote to Queen Victoria that the proposal to send the two princes on the same ship would cause public disquiet. Although he was her favourite prime minister, Disraeli got a very dusty answer. 'I entirely approve the plans for my grandsons, which should never have been put before the Cabinet.' As it happened, *Bacchante* was nearly wrecked in the Indian Ocean and only saved by a brilliant feat of seamanship on the part of the captain.

By the time the Easter holidays arrived Andrew had found another girlfriend at Gordonstoun. She was Clio Nathaniels, a seventeen-year-old brunette, who had only just started at the school. She was the friend of another girl, Sue Barnard, who was friendly with Andrew, but soon found herself displaced. Clio, the daughter of an architect who went with his wife after the war to live in the Bahamas, became the new favourite at the disco evenings and the Gordonstoun girls who were not in the Andrew set commented in a sprightly, bitchy way that she had become 'one of Andrew's harem'.

He was so taken with her that he got her invited for a weekend at Windsor Castle during the holidays. The North Warwickshire Hunt was putting on a cross-country and jumping event at Hatton near Warwick which Charles had arranged to see with Lady Sarah Spencer. Andrew decided he would like to go along too and bring Clio. It was a good outing, but Clio looked somewhat shy and embarrassed when the press photographers got to work.

The Queen and the family were gathering for the customary ritual of Badminton and Andrew drove there in his new blue Triumph Dolomite Sprint, which had been a birthday present from his mother and father. Andrew was using Badminton as his headquarters during his parachute course. He drove over to Brize Norton in Oxfordshire to report to Wing-Commander Jim Reynolds, the officer-in-charge of No. 1 Parachute Training School and went through the preliminary course in the training hangar. The next stage was a jump from a balloon, but high winds made this impossible for the time being, so Andrew drove back to Badminton and waited for the call. After three days conditions were good and Andrew got to the airfield early in the morning and made his first drop from 1,000 feet at 8.30 a.m. Prince Charles now joined him in the training hangar and the press was allowed to take pictures for it was wisely considered good publicity for the royal family and the services. So there were Charles and Andrew, suspended side by side in their harness, practising landings while a sergeant shouted instructions.

Then came the jumping from a Hercules transport plane. All went well and Charles, who had a tight schedule, completed the course as quickly as possible. But as Andrew was not in such a hurry and was showing himself supremely

Andrew leaves South Cerney airfield, Gloucestershire, after a thousand-foot parachute drop during which he had to twist his body seven times to untangle his lines. He passed the course and received his parachute insignia.

self-confident, permission was asked for television and press cameras to take pictures of him making a drop. This was granted and on Thursday, 19 April, Andrew came down out of the sky over the dropping zone at South Cerney, Gloucestershire. It was not without its drama. The parachute canopy opened but the lines became tangled. Andrew had to kick and twist his way out of trouble, spinning his body round seven times and dropping nearly 200 feet before he managed to free the tangled rigging. He made a safe landing taking forty-nine seconds to drop the 1,000 feet.

He is a cool customer. He collected his parachute according to the rule-book and walked away from the dropping-zone without fuss. Talking about the experience a few minutes later he said, 'Of course I was nervous. If you are not nervous you'll do something stupid.' Then he added, 'I am thoroughly enjoying all this and I'm dead keen to get up again. Parachuting is a feeling I would never have wanted to miss.' He did get up again the very same day. This time he jumped carrying a regulation fifty-five-pound pack. Afterwards he commented breezily: 'Carrying all this weight was a bit much. I had more difficulty getting into the plane than I did getting out.'

Wing-Commander Reynolds said later: 'Although his lines were twisted, he did exactly the drill he should have done. He had a very good parachute poise and a very good landing.' He added: 'Even if Prince Andrew's lines had remained twisted he would have landed safely enough because the parachute canopy was fully open.' All the same, it must have been a nasty few seconds, even for an experienced parachutist!

Andrew went on to complete the requisite number of drops and on 21 April received his RAF parachute insignia and certificate from Air Marshal Sir Alfred Ball, Acting Commander-in-Chief (Strike Command). He looked proud and happy – as he had reason to be. He could add his new badge to the ATC glider proficiency one he had earned two years previously. It was good going for a young man just over eighteen.

This year Andrew could look forward to another trip to Canada when the summer term was over. The Queen and Prince Philip were attending the Commonwealth Games in Edmonton which were being held from 3 to 12 August, and both Andrew and Edward had been invited along. Andrew went first to Ottawa, the Federal capital, and was treated as a favoured son. The Governor-General, Mr Jules Leger, gave a dinner and disco in his honour at the official residence, Rideau Hall. Over one hundred young people had been invited, including some of Andrew's friends from Lakefield, and the old early Victorian ballroom was swinging on its foundations by the end of the night. Andrew lived up to his reputation and charmed the girls, dancing with a succession of them, including

Lynn Nightingale, twenty-one, the talented Canadian figure-skating champion.

The Commonwealth Games, which are held every four years, take place traditionally in a friendly atmosphere, quite different from that of the Olympic Games where medals are fought for as if they were battle honours. For the most part, also, the competitors are amateurs in the old sense of the word – they do a job as well. There is rivalry and a desire to excel, but there survives a sense of fun and enjoyment and that is worthy of some comment in the modern sporting world. The Queen and Prince Philip, who have attended several of the Games, look forward to them and were glad this time to bring along Andrew and Edward.

Andrew had been to Edmonton briefly the previous year on his tour of Canada after Lakefield, but this time the city was *en fête*. It was very proud to have got the nomination for the Games and had cheerfully spent over £20 million on a new stadium seating forty-two thousand, a new aquatic centre and a velodrome. The city could afford this and more, for it lies in the centre of large oilfields which have brought considerable wealth to all classes of its near half-million inhabitants. It is a fine modern city, capital of Alberta which, apart from its oil and lumber, is one of the granaries of the world, and the gateway to the north with great new highways and comprehensive air links.

There was much for Andrew to see apart from the sports, for Edmonton had organized a great Festival of Arts and Culture to which many Commonwealth countries were contributing. There was a splendid Commonwealth carnival with Caribbean steel bands and African dancers. There were exhibitions of paintings and sculpture including the intricate, highly-developed arts of the Eskimos. There were concerts by the first-class Edmonton Philharmonic Orchestra with excellent singers and choirs. Added to all this there were parties, dances and discos.

It was a wonderful experience for Andrew and his young brother. They went out to the competitors' village at the fine university and had a meal in the canteen. Andrew went with Mr Pierre Trudeau to a Saturday night party at Darlings, the city's most fashionable disco, and a number of pretty girls went away with the memory of having danced with the dishy prince.

As well as the fun and the games, Andrew was sharing in the life of a great, new rich city in a country that could look forward to a splendid future of development. For this he could thank his parents and their position, but in return the experience was fitting him for his job. The crown is the unifying force of the Commonwealth and perhaps the Queen's greatest achievement has been to do everything in her power to knit together the many countries that now form the Commonwealth of Nations – no longer the British Commonwealth – which has in her reign replaced the old British Empire.

If it is to survive Andrew will have his part to play, just as much as his elder brother. Charles had his six months' educational experience in Australia, followed by a tour, and has since gone back several times as much for pleasure as to carry out duties. Australia likes him for himself and he likes Australians for themselves. Now Andrew is getting to know Canada and likes it. It seems fair to say that the Canadians, not a demonstrative people, like Andrew. The Queen and Prince Philip have shown wisdom in shaping the careers of their sons as they have grown up. First in Australia and now in Canada, one of their sons is known and liked. Charles and Andrew could not have achieved this if they were not young men of quality, but it has been good for the Crown and the Commonwealth – one might say for the British idea.

When Andrew was enjoying the pleasures of a great city in Edmonton, he was enjoying the fruits of a century of hard work and initiative by the men and women who chose Canada. Less than a century ago Edmonton was a settlement of around a thousand people living off the fur trade and a sawmill. In 1897 there was a gold rush to the North Saskatchewan River which flows through Edmonton. Later more prospectors came to the city en route for the Klondike. But it was black gold that made Edmonton, for in 1914 a huge find was made in the Turner Valley. Cree Indians and half-caste metis speaking French, men from far-off lands in search of black gold, pioneers in search of their own land – it is all almost within human memory in Edmonton. It is a stimulating story for a young man, such as Andrew, to hear. To go to these new countries even on a visit when you are young gives a new perspective to life which makes Europe seem small, distant and even provincial.

8

The Very Royal Navy

Back from Canada Andrew joined the family for the usual holiday at Balmoral. There was grouse-shooting on the newly-purchased 6,700-acre moors at Delnadamph, deer-stalking, fishing and swimming. Kirsty Richmond came to stay for a week, for she was now a welcome guest not only for Andrew but for the Queen and Prince Philip.

It was now time, however, for Andrew to discuss his future with his parents. He knew he would have to get down to his books if he wanted to get his three A-levels in the next year, 1979. It would be time enough, for he would be over nineteen. Charles had left Gordonstoun after taking his A-levels in the summer of 1967 when he was eighteen years and eight months and went to Trinity College, Cambridge, the same October, a month before he was nineteen. He had wanted to go to university before he did a spell in the services. His parents had agreed, partly because they knew that in two years' time, in 1969, he would be twenty-one and that it had been decided that he would be invested as Prince of Wales at a great ceremony in Caernarvon Castle. In preparation for the event Charles was to spend a term at the University of Wales in Aberystwyth learning Welsh and something of the history of the Principality. Charles would have found it difficult to combine service life with all these commitments.

At one time Andrew had also wanted to go to university before he too joined the services. There were strong rumours that he would be entered for Clare College at Cambridge. It would have been a feather in his cap if he had been accepted, for Clare has the brightest undergraduates in the university. Dr Ken Riley, senior tutor at the College, said bluntly: 'We're probably among the most stringent colleges as far as academic qualifications are concerned.' If Andrew had had such hopes, they were to be dashed. His parents decided that he would go straight into the Navy. It was announced that he would be applying for a twelve-year commission which meant that he would spend all his twenties in the service. He was to be trained not for general duties but as a helicopter pilot, which probably fitted in with his wishes.

The decision was momentous for the future of Andrew. It means that he will become a professional naval officer and that he may well take on further commitments after the completion of his twelve years – providing that he wants to and that the Navy wants him. A royal prince is given advantages and privileges which an ordinary officer would not be granted – however strenuous the official denials. No doubt Andrew will not be able to absent himself from his duties as often as Charles, who, as Prince of Wales, had many other calls on his time. But, after training, his postings will be carefully designed to ensure that his ship will be showing the flag in Commonwealth countries or where Britain wishes to preserve or promote its interests. To that extent Andrew will be employed to further the interests of the monarchy and of Britain.

Andrew has a character which will probably make him an excellent naval officer once he has accepted the discipline of the service. He may have had other ideas about his future, but probably he had little choice. The services provide a career for the royal sons which is safe, not necessarily physically, but politically. The strength of the monarchy is that it is above politics, both in Britain and in the Commonwealth. The services share, or should share, this quality, for their allegiance is to the crown. There was talk that one of the royal princes – Andrew seemed suitable – might be trained in the new technological skills which will transform industry, and thus give by his example a fillip to the men and women on whom the future will largely depend. But this would mean working in industry, perhaps by ability achieving a position of power, and this might entail political attitudes. It is far more acceptable for the royal princes to make a career in the services.

The choice of the Royal Navy was almost inevitable. Though now in size much inferior to the fleets of the United States and Russia, the Navy is still a power to be reckoned with, acts as a link with the worldwide Commonwealth, and enshrines hallowed national traditions. Apart from being the senior service it has also long been a favourite of the royal family.

But the links have never been closer, thanks to the influence of Prince Philip and his family. The two major events in Philip's youth which shaped his character were the years spent at Gordonstoun and in the Navy. He believes in Gordonstoun; he believes in the Royal Navy; it is as simple as that. He went into the Navy partially because his uncle, then Lord Louis Mountbatten, was in the service and could smooth the way for a nephew who was still at the time a foreign prince of Greece. But at the time Mountbatten was a junior officer, with his great days of glory in the Second World War ahead of him. There was a more illustrious Mountbatten for Philip to follow – his maternal grandfather.

His mother's father had been First Sea Lord at the outbreak of war in 1914. He was then Admiral His Serene Highness Prince Louis of Battenberg, to become later, when the family names and titles were changed, Louis Mountbatten, first Marquis of Milford Haven. How this German prince came to join the British Navy is a remarkable story – more remarkable than the story of how Prince Philip of Greece entered the same service.

Prince Louis as a boy was living in Darmstadt with his parents, Prince Alexander of Hesse and Princess Julie of Battenberg. His cousin, Louis, Grand Duke of Hesse, married Princess Alice, a daughter of Queen Victoria. One of her brothers, Prince Alfred, Duke of Edinburgh, made the Navy his career and in between commissions studied at Bonn University and visited his sister and her relatives in Darmstadt. Young Louis Battenberg listened to his stories of life in the British Navy and decided he wanted to make it his career. The choice of the British Navy for a young German prince may seem strange today, but at the time Germany had not been united and Prussia, the dominant power, had only a few warships in the Baltic. Louis's father suggested that the Austrian Navy, which operated through its Italian and Balkan possessions in the Mediterranean, might be a more suitable choice. But Louis was determined to join the British Navy, then at the height of its prestige and by far the largest fleet in the world. The powerful help of Prince Alfred was invoked and young Louis, who was a very bright boy, came to England at the age of fourteen, took British citizenship, passed the naval entrance easily and became a cadet. Normally he would have spent a year on a seagoing training ship, but Prince Alfred had arranged that he should join his own ship, HMS *Galatea*. However, Louis was to start his career in even more privileged company. The Prince of Wales, later Edward VII, was to make a cruise of the Mediterranean in the frigate *Ariadne*, and had Louis appointed to the ship. It is difficult to imagine a more splendid opportunity. Louis Battenberg, a mere cadet, accompanied the Prince and Princess of Wales on all the official visits – he went to Cairo and on sightseeing tours of the Nile with the Khedive, to Suez to inspect the not yet completed Canal, to Constantinople to visit the Sultan and to Athens to be entertained by the King and Queen of Greece (the King, George I, was a brother of the Princess of Wales). It was a brilliant start to a brilliant career. Louis was undoubtedly a very able man, and he was fortunate in that royal favour smoothed his path.

This then was the naval background that Andrew inherited through his father. On his mother's side the naval tradition was paramount. The Queen's father, George VI, his elder brother, Edward VIII (later Duke of Windsor) and his younger brother, George, Duke of Kent, all passed through the Royal Naval College at Dartmouth. George VI was never strong and his career as a young man was dogged by ill-health which finally forced him ashore from a service he had hoped as a younger son to make his life. He did, however, take part in the battle of

Jutland in 1916, bravely serving in the foremost gun-turret of the battleship, HMS *Collingwood*.

Their father, George V, spent fifteen years in the Navy and to him it was not so much a career as a calling. He joined as a naval cadet before he was thirteen with his elder brother, Prince Eddy, who was nearly fourteen. Eddy was the eldest son of the Prince of Wales (later Edward VII) so that in the normal course of events he would one day be King. Consequently he was only to do a few years in the Navy whereas George was to make it his career. Life on the training ship *Britannia* when they joined in 1877 was hard. George said many years later: 'It was a pretty tough place, and so far from making any allowances for our disadvantages the other boys made a point of taking it out of us on the grounds that they'd never be able to do it later on.' The training moulded his character and made him a fine officer imbued above all with a sense of duty; unfortunately, it made him a hard father to his sons.

But Prince Eddy died unexpectedly, bringing George in direct line to the throne, and his active career in the Navy was gradually brought to an end. Even so this career covered the critical years when the Navy had to be rapidly modernized and expanded to meet the threat from the new German fleet, and George's identification with the service at this time was good for both the nation and the monarchy.

In the generation before George it was Prince Alfred, Queen Victoria's second son, who made the Navy his career. He became a thoroughly professional officer and served for thirty-five years. From his early years he had always showed tremendous enthusiasm for the Navy. His father, Prince Albert, wrote: 'As regards his wish to enter the Navy, this is a passion which we his parents believe not to have the right to subdue. It is certainly not right to break the spontaneous desire of a young spirit.'

'Affie', as his mother called him, joined as a cadet at the age of fourteen, proved diligent and intelligent and went on to spend much of his life sailing the seas showing the flag during those long years of the Pax Britannica. It was an interesting time technically for the Navy was changing, rather slowly and at times reluctantly, from sail to steam, from wood to iron and from muzzle-loaders to shell-firing breech-loaders.

It was a time, never to be repeated, when every British naval officer seemed to the world to be surrounded by an aura of almost god-like power. The Royal Navy preserved peace on British terms sometimes by the appearance of one of its squadrons on the horizon, often by the mere threat of an appearance delivered by a British diplomat.

Alfred steadily rose in rank – accelerated by royal patronage – from Vice-Admiral to Admiral and finally Admiral of the Fleet. He commanded the Channel Squadron, was Commander-in-Chief of the Mediterranean Fleet and ended up as

Commander-in-Chief of Plymouth. When he was thirty he had married the Grand Duchess Marie, daughter of the Tsar Alexander II, who was blown up by a nihilists' bomb in 1881. Their daughter, Marie, married King Ferdinand of Roumania and in time their daughter, another Marie, married King Alexander of Yugoslavia. So Alfred was the progenitor of kings and queens of Balkan monarchies which were to disappear after the Second World War. He left the Navy in 1893 to succeed his uncle as Duke of Saxe-Coburg-Gotha and died of a heart attack in 1900 just before his fifty-sixth birthday. The Royal Navy had been his life and he had enjoyed it.

But of all the royal princes who have served in the Navy, the most endearing, in spite of his failings, was William, third son of George III, who in the end succeeded to the throne in 1830 at the age of sixty-four as William IV. Like Andrew he was a boisterous, independent boy when his father sent him away to sea in 1779 before he was fourteen. It was a time when the fortunes of Britain were at a very low ebb, largely due to the policies initiated by his father. The American colonies were in revolt. France and Spain saw their opportunity and declared war. The British were losing control of the seas and a great Franco-Spanish fleet was to sweep up the Channel in that summer of 1779. Britain was saved by a severe outbreak of sickness in the French fleet which forced it back to port. That winter Admiral Rodney was sent with a squadron to convoy provision ships to Gibraltar which was under heavy siege. The *Prince George*, with William on board, was part of the escort. It turned out to be a glorious mission. Off Finisterre fourteen Spanish supply ships were captured and then off Cape St Vincent Rodney destroyed a Spanish squadron of eleven battleships and three frigates. Young Prince William at the age of fourteen had taken part in one of the historic naval battles of British history. After provisioning Gibraltar Rodney sailed for the West Indies to meet the French fleet and sent the Spanish prizes back to Plymouth under an escort which included the *Prince George*.

After the fears of invasion England was triumphant. William was ordered to London to present the captured Spanish flags to his father. So it was that on 9 March 1780, less than a year after he had joined the Navy, William at a special court was introduced by the First Lord of the Admiralty to the King, handed over the flags and gave a report on the situation of beleaguered Gibraltar. It was the finest hour of his naval career.

William went on to lead a colourful life of dissipation, gambling and girls. He lost favour with the Navy for disobeying orders, and was not allowed to participate in the great battles of the day against the France of the Revolution. He had to follow the triumphant career of his great friend, Nelson, from the shore. But ironically he was promoted steadily during the war until in 1811 he became, by seniority, Admiral of the Fleet. Finally his brother, then George IV, gave him the ancient, honorific title of Lord High Admiral. William came to the throne in 1830 and reigned until 1837 when Victoria succeeded; he has gone down in British history as 'the Sailor King'.

With a naval background like this on both sides of the family Andrew was to feel at home when he went to Dartmouth – not that he finds any difficulty in making himself at home wherever he goes. His father talks about the Navy, his brother talks about the Navy, his great-uncle, Lord Mountbatten talked about the Navy.

Many of Andrew's ancestors served in the days when 'Britannia ruled the waves', but, though outmatched by the super-powers, the Royal Navy is still a force to be reckoned with and is undergoing what it calls 'the quiet revolution' which will equip it for the twenty-first century. In 1966 a twenty-year programme began which phased out the aircraft carriers and replaced them by five major new classes of surface ships and a much-improved nuclear submarine class. During Andrew's years of service the Navy will begin to reap the benefits of the invest-ment of money and brain-power. Within its limitations Britain will have, in the opinion of experts, a Navy of unsurpassed quality able to fulfil its commitments to NATO and also have a worldwide impact with its task forces. It is a prospect which would please those ancestors of Andrew from William to Alfred, Louis Battenberg and on to George V and George VI.

Andrew would be joining a fraternity of professionals. The First Sea Lord, Admiral Sir Terence Lewin, said recently:

The most heartening factor of all, however, remains the steadiness and thorough profes-sionalism of our officers and men ... I am sure that those of you who like myself have the good fortune to be in frequent contact with the young men who man our ships, submarines and aircraft today will agree with me that we have passed our trust into good hands.

When he went back to Gordonstoun in the autumn with Edward, Andrew was interviewed by his masters and told he would have to put his back into his studies if he was to pass his three A-levels the following summer. He took the advice seriously for he appreciated that failure would reflect not only on him, but on the family and the school.

The school broke new ground this term by appointing a girl as 'guardian' or senior prefect. She was Georgina Housman, eighteen, an outstanding girl who, with her twin sister, Lucilla, had been among the first thirty girls admitted to Gordonstoun in 1972, the year before Andrew arrived. There were now 120 girls among the 440 pupils.

Georgina, a vicar's daughter from Downham Market, Norfolk, is attractive, a good scholar and had represented the school at hockey, the traditional Gordonstoun game, and played for the north of Scotland. She was preparing for the Oxford scholarship entrance examination in classics.

In the Gordonstoun hierarchy laid down by the founder Hahn, the 'helpers' or 'colour-bearers' – the equivalent of prefects – are chosen by the pupils. The Guardian is selected from the helpers by the headmaster. The Guardian's role is different from that of the head boy or girl in an English school. It is to oversee the general welfare of all the pupils and to act as a link between them and the staff. Mr John Kempe, the headmaster, commented after Georgina's appointment: 'She has to keep in touch with me about what is going on and bring to my attention any problems. We have a short meeting every morning to discuss these things.'

Charles had been Guardian in his last year at Gordonstoun. So had Prince Philip. But the appointment of Georgina effectively eliminated Andrew from the honour. He was the colour-bearer – head boy – of his house in his final year 1978–9, but the headmaster considered Georgina a better choice as Guardian. There is no doubt she is an exceptional girl and her twin, Lucilla, is not far behind as head of her house.

Andrew worked at his books diligently that term, played rugby and hockey, found time to enjoy the friendship of the girls and looked forward to December when he would be taking his entrance tests for the Navy. As he was to be a helicopter pilot he reported first to the RAF Officers' and Air Crew Selection Centre for three days of physical and mental tests to see if he had the potential to be a naval pilot. The Centre is at the famous war-time fighter station at Biggin Hill and Andrew was met by the Commandant, Air Commodore Graham Smeaton. At the end of the three days he had, it is said, 'a glowing report'. He then went for interviews and further tests to a Royal Navy shore-based establishment, HMS *Daedalus* at Portsmouth. All went well there, but he was told he would have to wait a few months, like all the other applicants, before he was finally accepted. In his case, he could await the outcome with more confidence than the other candidates.

While Andrew was taking his tests, Princess Margaret's former husband, Lord Snowdon, got married again in the Kensington register office. His bride was Mrs Lucy Lindsey-Hogg, a television researcher whom he had known for some time. It removed Lord Snowdon another step away from the family which was no doubt a relief to him. He remains, however, a devoted father to the two children by his marriage to Princess Margaret, Viscount Linley and Lady Sarah Armstrong-Jones who have always been close to Andrew.

Before going to Windsor and Sandringham for Christmas and the New Year Andrew enjoyed a few days in London, shopping and going out with friends. It was noticed that, when he went the round the fashionable restaurants, such as Scott's in Mount Street, he bore himself very much as the self-confident young man-about-town.

January 1979 was a bad month in Britain. The weather was exceptionally severe and a series of strikes endangered food supplies and disrupted the hospital and ambulance services. Life at Sandringham went on as normal. Lady Sarah Spencer was a guest, so was her young sister, Lady Diana, aged seventeen. The girls had been through an anxious time for their father, Earl Spencer, a close friend of the Queen and the family, had suffered a severe cerebral haemorrhage in the autumn and, although he is only in his mid-fifties, his life had been in danger for some months. Charles was going off later to ski with Sarah at Klosters, and Diana was looked after by Andrew. Prince Philip took his three sons and their friends out on shooting parties in the freezing weather.

During the holiday Andrew asked his father if he could learn to fly in the Easter break and got permission. It was a privilege for him, as it meant that when he joined the Navy in the autumn he would get off to a 'flying start' compared with most of the other trainees.

He had not been back at school long when one of his girlfriends, Clio Nathaniels, had an emotional upset and ran away. She went to London, where her parents had friends, and then flew back to her home in Nassau. Her father said it was absolute nonsense that she had run away after a row with Andrew. Her mother, Elizabeth, who is an authoress, admitted that Andrew had been most embarrassed 'about the whole thing' and added, 'As far as I am aware Clio was only one of a number of friends'. Whatever the truth of the matter, Clio did not go back to Gordonstoun. On 19 February Andrew was nineteen and had the small celebration permitted to senior pupils at the school and then got on with his studies. In March he came down to Oxford for the Public School Hockey Festival as a member of the school team. Gordonstoun, who play in purple and white shirts, drew 3–3 against Charterhouse, but lost to Tonbridge 2–1. Then in April there was the Easter break and Andrew joined the family at Badminton, which has now been established as an annual royal ritual as firmly as Trooping the Colour and Ascot. Anne and Mark Phillips were competing in the Three-Day Event and did well this year – she was placed sixth and he third. The Queen had her fifty-third birthday and gave a party for the family and friends.

Andrew did not spend much time watching the horses for he was driving over nearly daily to an RAF airfield near Oxford for his flying lessons. He took ten lessons of forty-five minutes each over a fortnight and, on Friday, 13 April, had his first solo flight. He was flying an RN Chipmunk and after the six-minute flight his instructor, Commander Sandy Sinclair said he had done very well. After that he graduated to a twin-engined Beagle Basset of the Queen's Flight which had been acquired when Charles was learning to fly in 1970. It was now officially announced that he had been accepted by the Navy as a trainee helicopter pilot and would begin his training as a midshipman in September at the Royal Naval

Tatum O'Neal, the fourteen-year-old film star, had a royal turn-out for the London premiere of her new film *International Velvet* in July 1978. Here is Prince Andrew and with him were his brother Edward and his cousins, Viscount Linley and Lady Sarah Armstrong-Jones.

The Queen, Prince Philip and Prince Andrew wave at the crowds at London Airport on their departure for the Commonwealth Conference in Lusaka.

College, Dartmouth. His acceptance was not dependent on passing his A-levels as his O-levels were a sufficient qualification. Andrew would also be pleased to learn that he would be getting £2,400 a year during his training.

Andrew has been given an easier role in his naval career than Charles, who was asked to do a great deal in a very short time. Having left Cambridge Charles first underwent an advanced flying course with the RAF at Cranwell and then went to Dartmouth for an intensive shortened course with the Navy and was then promptly sent off to sea as an acting sub-lieutenant. As a seagoing officer in the modern technologically advanced service he was under great pressure, especially as he still had duties and responsibilities as Prince of Wales which, later in his career, he could only fulfil by long flights when his ship was, for example, in Far Eastern waters. Nevertheless he put in eighteen months' service at sea before training as a helicopter pilot, followed by a Royal Marine commando assault course. He was then posted to 845 Naval Air Squadron which did a tour of duty in the commando ship, HMS *Hermes*, in the Atlantic and West Indies. He came back and went to the Royal Naval College at Greenwich for the arduous three months' lieutenants' course. In 1976, his last year with the Navy, he was given command of HMS *Bronington*, a 360-ton minehunter with a complement of thirty-nine.

It is no wonder that Charles said: 'The trouble is people expect one to be a genius.' Charles is an eminently reasonable man, but it is easy to detect his feelings when he commented: 'The difficulty is that I did a shortened course of introduction to the navy and a fairly short period of training . . . I think now I've managed to accustom myself to the pace and made people realize I can't necessarily live up to the programme they've mapped out.'

With hindsight, there is no doubt that the programme mapped out for Charles by the naval authorities, presumably with the approval of Prince Philip, was an unnecessary strain. Andrew is to benefit from the experience for he will be taking a two-year course to train as a helicopter pilot without the need to acquire the considerable skills required today by a ship's officer.

When Andrew went to Dartmouth in September 1979, he joined the intake of supplementary list officers who will specialize in flying duties. The Navy accepts the need for specialization, but it is determined first to inculcate these future pilots into the traditions and attitudes of the service. They are drilled, disciplined and lectured so that first and foremost they will turn out naval officers with the training to understand and control men. This indoctrination period lasts seven months and if any fail to make the grade they will be weeded out at this stage.

In April 1980 the intake is being moved to Leeming in Yorkshire for general flying training on Bulldog aircraft. This course will last until October, when the successful will be awarded their wings. Once more, the failures will be weeded out.

Then follows the long, arduous training in helicopters at the Royal Naval Air

Station, Culdrose, in Cornwall. The first stage is to learn to fly the light, single-engined Gazelle. Then the young pilots graduate to the Sea King, used for anti-submarine duties, and the Wessex v, the troop-carrying assault helicopter. It is a tough course including submerged escape training, when crewmen are strapped into an old Wessex helicopter which is then turned over in a twenty-foot deep water-tank. The object of the exercise is to get out and swim to the surface, though there have been other macabre reasons given!

If you survive this course successfully, you are a fully-fledged naval helicopter pilot and will be posted to an operational squadron. And this is what Andrew is hoping to do at the end of the two-year course in the autumn of 1981 when he will be twenty-one and a half.

9

On Safari

On 16 May 1979 it was announced that the Queen and Prince Philip would be taking Andrew with them on a tour of Commonwealth countries in Africa during July and the beginning of August. Four countries were being visited – Tanzania, Malawi, Botswana and Zambia. In Lusaka, the capital of Zambia, the Queen, as Head of the Commonwealth, would be attending the opening of the Commonwealth Heads of Government Conference.

On one level this could be seen as a splendid holiday trip for Andrew at the end of his Gordonstoun years and before he joined the Navy in September. He had never visited Africa and would be seeing spectacular scenery and abundant wildlife in privileged circumstances. On a more serious level, the inclusion of Andrew in the royal party was a continuation of the Queen's policy of introducing her children to the Commonwealth as they grew up. In 1970, when Charles was twenty-one and Anne nineteen, they went with their parents on tours of Australia, New Zealand, Fiji and Tonga in the South Seas, and, later in the year, Canada.

As it turned out, however, Andrew was to take part in the most remarkable Commonwealth tour of the Queen's reign so far, which started with controversy and ended in triumph. After his years of studying history in textbooks and taking part in make-believe exercises as a member of the school cadet force, Andrew had an opportunity of seeing history being made against the background of a bloody war which was for real. How much he took in is difficult to say. But he is a lively, intelligent young man of nineteen and the opportunity to learn was there, with his mother playing a considerable part.

Lusaka lies not far from the border between Zambia and Rhodesia, the latter a self-governing British colony which severed its allegiance in 1964 with a Unilateral Declaration of Independence (UDI) because the dominant white minority refused to extend political rights to the black majority. Since then an increasingly bitter war had been waged between the white-led armed forces and the guerrilla fighters of the Patriotic Front, based in Zambia and Mozambique. With the help of its powerful southern neighbour, South Africa, Rhodesia had for years survived sanctions and warfare. Several attempts were made to settle the dispute, but all failed, including that by Mr Henry Kissinger when he was the American Secretary of State.

Finally in 1979 Mr Ian Smith, who led the white Rhodesian Government with stubbornness and skill, put through an internal settlement. A new constitution was proclaimed which gave the vote to the black majority, elections were held, a black government was installed under Bishop Muzorewa and even the name of the country was changed to Zimbabwe-Rhodesia.

But peace did not come. The black African states, supported by most of the Commonwealth and world opinion, decided that the new constitution was only a cosmetic exercise and that the white minority still retained effective power by controlling the armed forces, the police, the judiciary and senior administration – and what is more had a veto on constitutional changes.

In Britain a section of the Conservative Party had always been sympathetic to the white Rhodesians and in May of 1979 it was greatly heartened by the result of the general election. The Conservatives defeated Labour by a handsome margin on a policy considerably more right-wing than the country had been offered for years. The redoubtable Mrs Margaret Thatcher became Prime Minister and it was believed she was in favour of the new settlement in Zimbabwe-Rhodesia.

Everyone knew that the Rhodesian problem would dominate the Conference in Lusaka. There seemed a real danger that, if Britain favoured Zimbabwe-Rhodesia, the Commonwealth, now numbering forty-one independent states throughout the world, would be in peril.

The Queen was only too aware of this. It is insufficiently appreciated by the people of Britain how much work the Queen has done to build the Commonwealth, which has arisen out of the ashes of the old British Empire. In the Christmas broadcast after her Coronation in 1953 she said of the then embryonic Commonwealth: 'To that conception of an equal partnership of nations and races I shall give myself heart and soul every day of my life.' For twenty-six years she has done just that.

As a young woman she travelled, listening and observing. As the years passed she greeted new members of the Commonwealth and was able not just to listen, but quietly to give the benefit of her growing experience. The media has reported her tours giving accounts of her clothes and her public appearances. It has seemed scarcely conscious of her growing influence on a world-scale.

In her methodical, determined way the Queen has stored up her knowledge of countries and the personalities of those who have been called to rule them. She has seen their triumphs and disasters, shared their happiness and sorrow. Politicians have come and gone, but the Queen goes on, a stable force in a changing world. The British naturally look on Elizabeth as *their* Queen. It is difficult for them to grasp the position she has created as Head of the Commonwealth, which at times

During the great African tour in July/August 1979 Prince Andrew was given the opportunity of seeing his mother receive a triumphant welcome as Head of the Commonwealth at the meeting of Commonwealth Heads of Government in Lusaka, the capital of Zambia.

At Cowes, August 1979, Andrew sails in one of the Flying Fifteen class which his father, Prince Philip, has done much to popularize.

must make the affairs of Britain seem, if not provincial, at any rate not exclusively important.

This, then, was the background to the 1979 Lusaka Conference which Andrew would be watching as the second son of the Queen.

Towards the end of June and at the beginning of July Andrew, up at Gordonstoun battling with his three A-levels, must have wondered at times whether the African tour would take place at all. A skilful campaign was mounted to stop the Queen going to Lusaka as part of a wider plan to prevent the conference taking place there at all. The white-led Rhodesian forces stepped up their bombing raids on the Patriotic Front camps around Lusaka and made a daring helicopter-borne infantry attack on its headquarters in the suburbs of the city. The casualties were numerous and the atmosphere in the area heavy with anger at the lack of adequate defence.

In London the friends of the white Rhodesians spread the view that it would be unsafe for the Queen to go to Lusaka. A story was invented that alternative arrangements were already being made to change the venue to Nairobi, well to the north in Kenya. This was indignantly denied by Mr Ramphal, the Commonwealth Secretary-General, who has his headquarters in London. He spoke of a malicious campaign in the press. It certainly had success, for it spread to the world media and Mrs Thatcher, on a short visit to Australia, was asked at a press conference about the safety of the Queen at Lusaka. She replied that she would 'advise' her about the visit when she had studied the security reports being prepared.

This remark by the Prime Minister was the cause of a quite remarkable conflict of wills between her and the Queen. As a constitutional monarch the Queen is obliged, in the final analysis, to accept the 'advice' (a euphemistic term for 'decision') of the government of the day in all matters of public policy. But it is a nice constitutional point whether the Queen is obliged to accept the advice of the government in matters affecting her duties as Head of the Commonwealth, a postwar title, enacted by Parliament, accepted by the countries of the Commonwealth, and residing in the monarch personally.

To the Queen, who has devoted her life to the Commonwealth and who believed she could make a contribution to a solution of the Rhodesian problem during her talks with leaders in Lusaka and elsewhere, it was galling to be told she would have to await advice for permission to attend. In her reign she has seen prime ministers, some good, some bad, come and go. Mrs Thatcher had only just been brought to power and had little or no experience of world affairs. Judging from comments made by Buckingham Palace, the Queen was quite aware how the safety scare had been contrived and, in any case, has spent her life at the mercy of cranks or terrorists who might endanger her life at any public appearance.

The media in Britain tried to play down the difference of opinion between Palace and No. 10 Downing Street because it did not wish to create a constitutional crisis between a dearly loved Queen and a Conservative prime minister whom for the most part it had helped to bring to power.

But the story kept breaking out. Mrs Thatcher stuck to what she considered her constitutional rights to give advice which would have to be obeyed. The Palace, increasingly irritated, let it be known that any advice against going would be accepted only as 'a last resort'. It became clear that the Queen would be reluctant to accept the advice of Mrs Thatcher alone. Senior cabinet ministers and other Commonwealth leaders would have to be consulted.

Mrs Thatcher said in the House of Commons on 3 July that in tendering advice, 'I have to wait to the last minute to receive the latest, up-to-date reports'. The use of the phrase 'at the last minute' was not well received at the Palace. The security reports were finally completed and examined. They said that the Queen would be in no more danger on this trip than on others she had made. It now seemed virtually certain that the Queen would make the trip with Mrs Thatcher's approval. But she did wait to the last minute to give it. The Queen was leaving for Africa on Thursday, 19 July. On the previous Tuesday, the seventeenth, Mrs Thatcher said in a written Commons reply that, after deep and careful consideration, she had concluded that it was not necessary for her to advise the Queen against going. On the same Tuesday evening Mrs Thatcher had one of her regular audiences with the Queen. Unfortunately, one can only surmise the atmosphere!

Out of the affair Mrs Thatcher may well have thought that she had shown who was boss. But the Palace has long memories.

Andrew had finished at Gordonstoun on the same Tuesday and came down to London to get ready for Africa and read some of the excellent material which is prepared by the royal staff to brief the family on the countries they are visiting and the personalities they will meet.

It must have been with feelings of relief that the royal party finally set off on Thursday, 19 July from London Airport on the first leg of the tour. The Queen travels in great style. Her aircraft, an RAF VC10, had been converted into a number of comfortable apartments and the food and refreshment for the family and the senior members of the entourage were of a royal standard. A second aircraft carried the luggage and the rest of the staff.

The plane landed in the evening at Kilimanjaro International Airport in Northern Tanzania and the royal party went by car to a lodge at Arusha, a pleasant town in the foothills of Mount Meru surrounded by fertile land and herds of cattle. For Andrew it was a splendid introduction to Africa. Arusha lies in the shadow of Kilimanjaro, Africa's highest mountain at 19,340 feet, whose snow-capped peak, three degrees south of the Equator, seems to defy reason. The Arusha National Park is not as spectacular as that of Serengeti to the west, with its huge herds of plains animals and accompanying prides of lions, but it has much to offer – elephants, giraffes, black rhinos, hippos, buffalo, waterbucks, baboons and leopards.

The next day the royal family flew to Dar-es-Salaam, the capital, and was greeted by President Nyerere, fifty-eight, silver-haired, the founding father of Tanzania which was granted its independence by Britain in 1961. The drums beat out a welcome; groups of women dancers swirled and clapped their hands; there was a spray of frangipani for the Queen and the President put his hand to her elbow as she stepped up to the dais to be greeted as, 'Queen of England, Great Britain and Northern Ireland, Head of the Commonwealth'. She knows the President well, for he has paid a state visit to Britain and has attended many Commonwealth conferences. Prince Philip opened the country's first Parliament back in December 1961. Andrew looked very smart in a grey suit, smiled, shook numerous hands and asked intelligent questions.

On the drive to State House he was able to see how much the visit meant to Tanzania. The crowds were waving Union Jacks specially flown in from Britain; schoolchildren were there in their thousands, the girls neat in white blouses and blue skirts; on the arrival a choir sang a song which had been specially composed, 'Peace in the Commonwealth'; in State House where the party was staying the rooms were filled with roses brought from the mountains.

There was a walk-about in the city, which has a delightful harbour front where the buildings show the influence of Arabs, Germans (it was once a German colony), Indians and the British. The British wives were standing in a group with a banner for Andrew, 'Hi! Andy come and have coffee'.

In the afternoon an Andover of the Queen's flight, which had been flown from Britain for the short trips, flew the party to the island of Zanzibar, once a centre of the Arab slave trade which Britain put down in the nineteenth century. They walked along the main street with its graceful Arab architecture and watched more groups of girls dancing in their honour.

After all this colourful sightseeing the evening was given over to more serious matters. President Nyerere gave a banquet at which the Queen appeared in green chiffon with a tiara and necklace of diamonds. Andrew was able to watch how warmly the Tanzanian élite, leaders of an avowedly Socialist state, felt towards his mother. He was also able to appreciate when she made her speech how warmly she felt, not only to the company in the room, but to the aspirations of black Africa. 'Freedom', she said, 'can only exist where there is no fear of oppression and injustice, and no constant dread of death or disablement brought by poverty, starvation and disease.' She went on:

I am confident that the Lusaka Conference will demonstrate the Commonwealth's deep concern about the freedom of the individual wherever this is denied or threatened – whether by oppressive regimes or by the harshness of economic circumstances, and the failure of others more fortunate to provide the help that is needed.

It was as near as the Queen could go in a public speech to comment on Rhodesia and its neighbour, South Africa, resolutely pursuing its policy of apartheid. But in talks with President Nyerere that day and the next she was able to discuss the forthcoming Conference. He was the organizing brain behind the 'Five Front Line States' – Tanzania, Zambia, Botswana, Angola and Mozambique – which were most closely concerned with the independence struggle.

On Saturday the Queen was informed that the previous day Rhodesian forces had carried out a raid with troops and aircraft on a Patriotic Front supply camp near Livingstone, just inside the Zambian frontier. The Press Secretary, Mr Michael Shea, was instructed to tell the press that the raid was no reason for the Queen's visit to be altered in any way.

During Saturday the royal party flew back to the Kilimanjaro area and Andrew was able to spend some time in the game reserves. The Queen visited agricultural centres and toured the Kilimanjaro Christian Medical Centre and spent most time in the children's wards. On Sunday the royal party flew off to Blantyre in Malawi. The Tanzanian trip had been a great success personally, but not without anxiety for the Queen. Nyerere had made clear that if Britain recognized Zimbabwe-Rhodesia, Tanzania would probably leave the Commonwealth.

Andrew would know from his briefing material that Blantyre was named after the birthplace in Scotland of David Livingstone, for he explored the area in the mid-nineteenth century, found it riven by tribal wars and a prey to slave-traders and came back to arouse the conscience of Britain. Malawi – Nyasaland before its independence in 1963 – still retains the influence of the many Scottish missionaries who answered the call, even to strict rules of dress and public decorum.

The airport at Blantyre is set among mountains and at this time of the year their slopes are ablaze with red jasmine, poinsettias and oleanders. There to greet the Queen, Prince Philip and Andrew was one of the most remarkable rulers of new Africa, Dr Hastings Banda, wearing a black homburg and dark glasses, a fly whisk in one hand and an ivory cane in the other. He is seventy-seven, a son of a peasant family of the country, who worked in South Africa, studied medicine in the United States, took further diplomas in Scotland and practised as a doctor on Tyneside for the Mission for Coloured Seamen. It was not until 1958, when he was fifty-six, that Banda was persuaded to return to what was then still Nyasaland.

In the struggle for independence Dr Banda was imprisoned, but led the country to freedom and has dominated the political life of the country ever since with apparently no opposition. He has been President for life since 1970. He is a conservative with a great admiration for British traditions and the monarchy, and has fallen out with the neighbouring black states by developing trade links with South Africa and accepting its aid. 'I would do business', he has said, 'with the devil to help the economic development of Malawi.' In fact, under his rule Malawi has prospered, helped by good prices for its tea and coffee. He is authoritarian, censors the press, relies for support on the well-organized 'League of Women' and makes life worthwhile for the British expatriates who supply management and technological skills.

Andrew, waiting behind the Queen and Prince Philip, watched Dr Banda coming to greet them, smiling and pleased. This was the second founding father of an African state Andrew had met – others were to follow before the tour was over. Andrew, who up to now had seen his mother at decorous ceremonies in England and Scotland, now saw how she entered into the spirit of an African welcome as Dr Banda danced along the red carpet with the Queen as the band played its infectious music and she waved her hand in time with the rhythm. She often seems to relax more easily in these new countries of the Commonwealth.

The next day it was on to Lilongwe, the new capital that has been built since independence. There is still much to be done, but it is already a handsome, widely-spaced city with handsome buildings. Andrew was able to share in the most spectacular welcome so far in the tour. There were thousands of women in native costume, dancing, clapping, crying out in high-pitched voices, 'Eliz-zabeth, Eliz-zabeth, God Save Our Queen'.

The drums thundered as the Queen inspected the immaculate guard of honour and then she and Prince Philip passed on to the fearsome group of chanting warriors wearing lions' teeth and leopard skins with bells on their ankles and carrying hide shields. All this is now just a part of folk tradition, like Highland dress and dancing, for many of the dancing warriors were civil servants or veterans of the King's Own African Rifles who served in Ethiopia, India and Burma in the last war and barked out their regimental numbers proudly to Prince Philip. Many thousands of black people throughout East Africa served in the regiment and later in the day the Queen laid a wreath on the Cenotaph in Lilongwe while choirs of women softly sang a lament.

The warriors had in that war gone to fight the Japanese in the jungles of Burma when Malawi was a colony of the British Empire. Andrew could reflect that it is due partly to his mother's work as Head of the Commonwealth that the citizens of an independent country want her to come amongst them as a friend, sharing their past and their hopes for the future.

There were ceremonies and receptions all that day, but there followed, on

Tuesday, 24 July, a day of rest up on the high Zomba plateau with its sparkling air, surrounded by the Shire Highlands and forests of sweet-smelling eucalyptus and pine. There are cool streams and pools where trout are plentiful. It is a lovely place and the royal party stayed in a stone-built house built in the English style with glorious views of mountain and plain not far from Zomba, the old capital, where a British botanist founded a Botanical Garden. Now that the capital has moved to Lilongwe, the new University of Malawi has taken over the old adminis-trative buildings.

In the centre of Africa a sense of peace can fall that is deeper than in even the remote areas of Europe – there are times when a soothing hand seems to give a tranquillity not of this world to body and mind. It is the magic of Africa and on the Zomba plateau it is pervading. The Queen rested and read her briefings for the Lusaka conference. Prince Philip cooked sausages for a barbecue lunch. Andrew was able to wander at will.

The next day the royal aircraft took off for Gaborones, the capital of Botswana, a vast, thinly-populated country, mainly covered by the Kalahari Desert. It was a long flight for a great detour had to be made to avoid Rhodesian airspace, but there was a great welcome at the airport with swirling bare-breasted girl dancers and high-pitched screams of '*Pula*' – which means rain and in arid Botswana is as traditional a welcome as 'Greetings' or '*Salaam*'. The President, Sir Seretse Khama, was there to greet the Queen and her husband and son; with him was Lady Khama, an Englishwoman whom he had met in London and fallen in love with, when she was an ordinary middle-class girl, Ruth Williams, and he was studying law in the Middle Temple after some years at Balliol College, Oxford.

When Andrew shook hands with them, he was meeting two people who had braved much for love. Seretse Khama of the royal house of the Bamangwato inherited the Chieftaincy at the age of four in 1925. While his uncle acted as regent, Seretse studied first in South Africa before coming to England. When he took Ruth back home there was opposition from the tribe because she was white, but the elders declared in his favour and gradually opposition died down. But then the British Government decided in 1950 to hold an enquiry into his fitness for office and he was summoned to London. Finally he was told he must renounce his Chieftaincy and would be offered a modest pension to live in Britain. He refused and was then told he was banished from his country. It is believed that pressure had been brought by the South Africans on the British Government to depose Seretse as they could not tolerate a powerful Chief of a country bordering their own who was married to a white woman. For six years Seretse and his wife lived in exile, but were finally allowed back to allay mounting popular agitation for his return. The British were by now preparing the country for independence and Seretse went into politics and became a leading figure. When the first general election was held in 1965 Seretse became Prime Minister and in the following year, when Botswana became independent, President.

Now in July 1979, when the Queen inspected the guard of honour at the airport of Gaborones, she was escorted by the eldest son of Seretse and Ruth, Brigadier Ian Khama. There were friendly crowds, waving and shouting, on the drive into town and one large sign reading '*Garokang ka Pula*' [Come with rain] to impress that word '*Pula*' on the royal party. There was a banquet in the evening and once more the Queen was able to have confidential talks on the forthcoming conference with another African ruler who is closely concerned with the Rhodesian problem. Botswana has enormously long frontiers with both South Africa and Rhodesia. Thousands of black Rhodesians have made their way to Botswana en route for refugee or guerrilla training camps in Zambia. From time to time the Rhodesian forces launch raids across the frontier. But with South Africa Botswana continues to have almost normal relations. Many Botswana people work for a time in South Africa. In return South Africa buys large quantities of carcasses from the great herds of cattle which are the principal source of Botswana's income.

These trade links were very evident when the royal party arrived at Gaborones, for the town was full of South African businessmen who had come for the annual Trade Fair which the Queen was to open on the second day of her visit. This turned out to be a very jolly affair – an African variation on the Agricultural Shows which always absorb the Queen and Prince Philip when they visit them in Britain. There were hundreds of children who shrieked and danced a welcome to the Queen's delight; the South African visitors could not contain their curiosity and, in many cases, their evident pleasure. '*Pula*,' said the Queen as she opened her speech, which made the crowd roar with appreciation.

When the royal planes took off for Zambia, they flew for a time near the South African border and Andrew may have recalled that it was in this area that one of his contemporaries at Gordonstoun had been shot dead the previous year. Nicholas Love, eighteen, had been on an adventure holiday and was with two South African companions who were game-rangers when they crossed the ill-defined border and were picked up by a Botswana patrol. There was a tragic misunderstanding and the patrol opened fire. After an enquiry there were apologies and the affair was smoothed over, but too late for a promising youngster.

At Lusaka there was perhaps the greatest welcome of the tour – there was happiness in the air as the Queen, followed by Prince Philip and Andrew, stepped from the plane. The crowds waved Union Jacks and screamed 'Queenie', as a beaming 'K.K.' – President Kenneth Kaunda – came forward to greet the visitors. The military band played the national anthems; the guard of honour was inspected and then merriment took over. Everyone seemed to be laughing, shouting and waving as if it was a joyous carnival.

But as they drove away through the crowds, the Queen and her family passed banners, such as 'No sell-out by Britain on Zimbabwe', which heralded the problems of the days ahead.

Kenneth Kaunda was the fourth founding father of a new African state whom Andrew had now met on this tour. There had been Nyerere, the Catholic-educated Socialist intellectual, Hastings Banda, the conservative pragmatist, and Seretse Khama, the proud aristocrat. K.K. is somebody very special. He radiates a certain spiritual power which springs from his deep commitment to Christianity. Now fifty-five, he was born in a Church of Scotland Mission in the Northern Province of what was then Northern Rhodesia. His father was an ordained priest who had become a teacher. His mother was one of the first African women teachers in the territory. K.K. in turn became a teacher, but by 1950 was an active political worker and in a few years established himself as the most effective leader of the movement for independence. He was imprisoned for two months and then made a long tour of India where he was very ill with tuberculosis. He came back, was imprisoned again for nine months, came out and saw with dismay as a believer in non-violence that the situation was explosive. But the struggle for independence was to end in peaceful victory in October, 1964 when K.K. became the first President of the new Zambia. Even at that proud moment he remained quietly modest. Since then he has had to battle with many problems, some embittering, but he remains a man of ideals which are rooted in Christian faith.

The next day a visit was paid to Kitwe up in the north by the borders of Zaïre (previously the Belgian Congo). With nearby Ndola, Kitwe is at the centre of the copperbelt whose mineral riches are the foundation of the Zambian economy. Kitwe bears no comparison to the old mining villages of Britain. It is a pleasant town where tropical flowers give colour to the avenues where the expatriate miners and managers, mainly South African and British, live with their families in spacious bungalows surrounded by lawns where water sprinklers play. The black workers live in reasonable comfort and there is an air of prosperity even though the price of copper has been depressed for some time by world conditions.

The Queen talked to the British community, but was able to see around her banners prepared by the black population greeting her with charming grace: 'The Queen is the strong symbol of love and radiance in the democratic world.' In the afternoon it was back to a state banquet given by the President in honour of the Queen. Zambia was going through a bad time economically, partly due to the Rhodesian situation, but money had been found to put on a good show for the Conference. Wines and spirits, fresh fruits, toiletries and other luxuries were available for the visiting delegations and journalists. It was a question of national pride to put on a good show. If there were any shortages of the amenities of life, it was the journalists from London who seemed to grumble the most as if their daily standard of life was of a Savoy Hotel or Ritz quality.

The next day was a Sunday (29 July). In the morning the Queen, with Prince Philip and Andrew, attended communion service in the Cathedral of the Holy Cross with the President and Mrs Kaunda, who have a family of seven sons and two daughters. Later there was a reception for the quite numerous British community at which Prince Philip and Andrew were kept busy talking to the wives of the diplomats, businessmen and technicians stationed in Zambia. Then the family flew off to the Luangwa Valley, six hundred miles to the east, which is largely preserved as a national park where the wildlife compares with any in East Africa. They were to stay there for a day making trips from a very comfortable lodge in Range-Rovers. The African bush has been described as 'exquisitely boring', but for a few magic minutes at dawn and sunset the land is bathed in gold and purple so it was to be expected that the family was up and about to see the dawn. The Queen relaxed in trousers and a shirt, Prince Philip and Andrew in equally casual dress. Luangwa is famous for its huge herds of elephants and buffalos, but there are hippos, black rhinos, zebras, many types of antelopes with their accompanying predators, lions (some black-maned) and leopards.

The Queen and Prince Philip have visited many great game-reserves in their lives, but for Andrew this tour had the magic of a first experience. But on Monday evening it was back to Lusaka for more serious matters. The Commonwealth Conference was to open on Wednesday, 1 August, and although the Queen does not attend she would be busy greeting the heads of government and conducting private talks. Mrs Thatcher and Lord Carrington, the Foreign Secretary, had arrived on Monday. She arrived to a bad press, whilst Andrew could read in the Zambia *Daily Mail* praise of his mother calculated to turn almost any head. The editorial said that the Queen, who could quite easily be elected Queen of the World, made a complete contrast with Mrs Thatcher, the racist. It added that the Queen had 'an extraordinary loving heart' for every human being, regardless of colour.

If this trip had given Andrew his first views of African wildlife, he was now to see in Lusaka for the first time in his life a city teeming with another form of life – not wild, but potentially more dangerous – hundreds of politicians, diplomats and journalists from all over the world. Lusaka is not a large city, so that it seemed to have been taken over as the members of thirty-nine Commonwealth delegations moved around the centre with their documents, the television crews set up their cameras and the journalists sped from one briefing to another. For a few days Lusaka was the political centre of the world: the Americans, who had tried so hard to settle the Rhodesian problem, were there in force, and the Russians and the

Iron Curtain countries, who had more than one finger in the pie, were there to keep informed.

There were receptions and dinners, talks behind closed doors, press conferences, rumours and denials. Nigeria announced on Tuesday evening that it was nationalizing British Petroleum's considerable oil interests there. Lord Carrington had a stand-up row about it with the Nigerian Foreign Minister the next day on the lawns of the British Embassy – in full public view. The Queen went on having talks at her villa and gave luncheon parties which she hoped would be helpful. Mr Malcolm Fraser, the new young Conservative Prime Minister of Australia, was making a name for himself as a skilful mediator. Mr Michael Manley, Prime Minister of Jamaica since 1972, was also playing a role behind the scenes.

On 1 August President Kaunda, as host and chairman, opened the Conference. The Queen's work was nearly over. It was now time for the political leaders to get to work.

Andrew and his father had a day off from diplomacy and politics when they went to a meeting at a large farm held to launch a campaign to save the rhino. It is faced with extinction because the animals are killed for their horns which fetch great prices in the Middle and Far East where they are ground to a powder used as an aphrodisiac. Prince Philip made a light-hearted speech saying that drastic measures should be taken to protect the rhinos from poachers, adding, 'there will be a lot of frustrated customers for the horns'.

In the evening, however, they were back on duty at the banquet given by the Queen for all the heads of delegation. It was the climax of the tour. It was a great occasion for Andrew to watch his mother, in an ice-blue evening gown, with a sapphire and diamond tiara with matching necklace and ear-rings, receive the representatives of the Commonwealth she has devoted her life to build.

That night Prince Philip left for London to keep an appointment. During the next day Andrew, in bush jacket and jeans, went off on a local safari with a group of young men which included Kaweche, one of President Kaunda's sons who is the same age as he, nineteen. The Queen had a few more talks, but they were taking on a farewell note. 'The Queen is really a godlike figure,' said one African politician, 'a sort of problem-solving umpire. This is where her role is so vital to the Commonwealth countries.'

The Queen and Prince Andrew flew back to London on Saturday, 4 August, with memories of crowds at the airport crying, 'Bye-bye, Queenie', and President Kaunda waving his handkerchief as the plane sped down the runway. 'During this last week,' the Queen had said, 'I have received a wonderful welcome which I shall always remember.'

The Lusaka Conference went on to produce a plan to settle the Rhodesian situation which this time everyone fervently hoped would be a success. Mrs Thatcher in a few days found herself praised and fêted as she put forward the British proposal for a conference in London to hammer out a constitution acceptable to Bishop Muzorewa's government and the Patriotic Front. How great a part the Queen had played in creating the atmosphere of friendly co-operation that made the Conference a success will probably remain a secret for many years, but one of her advisers said as she left Lusaka that the visit had been a triumph. 'But the Queen would never boast about this,' he added. 'It is not in her nature.' All the talk about the Queen's safety being endangered by going to Lusaka had been made to look nonsense.

For Andrew the tour had combined pleasure and the opportunity to see his mother in a new light – the experienced, skilful Head of the Commonwealth working hard to bring peace and prosperity. He had seen magnificent scenery and abundant wildlife, but he had also had the opportunity of meeting the men who are creating a new Africa. Those days with his mother and father cannot but have deepened his understanding of the opportunities that lie ahead for him if he wishes to use them.

Back in England, while the Queen was clearing up business that had accumulated, Andrew went down to the Isle of Wight to join his father and his brothers, Charles and Edward, on the royal yacht for the opening of Cowes Week. Charles introduced Andrew to wind-surfing, a sport he had tried out at Cowes the previous year. It is a very wet sport for it consists of riding the water on a surf board and holding on to a small sail and attempting to guide it with the hands. Charles proved quite expert, but Andrew was as much in the water as out. He decided to get his revenge. With a girlfriend he took out a speed-boat and weaved it round Charles on his surf board doing his best to upset him.

Andrew crewed in a Flying Fifteen race, while Prince Philip took Edward in another craft. But the sailing was not to last long this year, for on the Wednesday the Queen arrived and the family set off in the *Britannia* for a cruise of the Western Isles before going to Balmoral for the summer holiday. Princess Anne arrived for the cruise and so did Princess Alexandra and her husband, Mr Angus Ogilvy.

Up at Balmoral Andrew learned towards the end of August that he had passed all three of his A-levels. It was a good result for it showed that in spite of all his outside interests he had worked at his books. It was also another sign that Prince Philip's sons were bright. After a shaky start Charles had done well at Gordonstoun and Cambridge. It marked quite a change in the royal family for George VI, his elder brother, Edward VIII (later the Duke of Windsor) and their father, George V, had all been poor scholars.

There was, however, not to be much time for Andrew and his family to enjoy

The mourning for the murdered Lord Mountbatten by his family, the nation and the world in Westminster Abbey on 5 September 1979. Andrew, wearing his midshipman's uniform, takes his place in the sombre procession.

The Andrew look of fun when he entered the Royal Naval College at Dartmouth on 12 September 1979 to train as a helicopter pilot. He seems to have broken the ice with Captain Nicholas Hunt, the commander of the College.

their holiday this year. Within a few days – on Bank Holiday Monday, 27 August – came the news that Lord Mountbatten and several members of his family had been murdered by the IRA when a remote-controlled bomb blew up their boat just off the coast in Donegal Bay. They had been on holiday in the Republic of Ireland.

Mountbatten was killed instantly with a grandson, Nicholas Knatchbull, and a young local boy who was helping with the lobster-potting. The Dowager Lady Brabourne, the mother of Lord Brabourne, married to Mountbatten's elder daughter Patricia, died soon after. Lord and Lady Brabourne and another of their sons were severely injured.

On that same black Monday eighteen members of the Army were killed in an IRA ambush just inside the Ulster border, the largest number of casualties to be sustained by the services in one incident since the troubles had started again ten years before.

The nation was first stunned and then, in the way of the British, quietly, but deeply angry.

For the royal family it was a bitter blow. Charles has described his great-uncle as the centre of the family. 'Certainly Lord Mountbatten has had an influence on my life and I admire him, I think, almost more than anybody else. He's a very great man.'

The royal family was somewhat scattered when the news came. Andrew and Edward were with their mother at Balmoral; Charles was in Iceland at Lord Tryon's fishing lodge, and Prince Philip was in France on his way to an equestrian event in Normandy.

It was for the Prime Minister, Mrs Thatcher, and her government to deal with the political implications. For the family, soon reunited at Balmoral, it was a time for grief. It seemed a blow to natural justice that a man, already old (he was seventy-nine) and enjoying a well-earned retirement after a life of great achievement and heroism, should end in such a despicable way.

Lord Mountbatten had, with his usual panache and love of pageantry, meticulously organized his funeral as he grew old. In this he followed the example of Sir Winston Churchill. Both had wanted their passing to be commemorated in such a way that the nation should rejoice in its traditions and renew its unity.

So it turned out on Wednesday, 5 September 1979, when a great funeral service was held at Westminster Abbey after a magnificent military procession had escorted the coffin of Lord Mountbatten through the heart of London from the Chapel Royal at St James's Palace. Prince Philip and Charles followed the gun-carriage, drawn by sailors, in naval uniform. Andrew, wearing for the first time in public his uniform as a midshipman, was in the Abbey with the Queen and the rest of the family. For him it was his first experience of a great state occasion of such solemn magnificence. The kings and queens, princes and princesses from other countries were in most cases related to Mountbatten and so to him. But through its special representatives and ambassadors the whole world was there to pay tribute to a man who had served his country with immense distinction in war and peace.

The impeccably organized events of the day, seen by tens of millions on television, achieved the purpose that Mountbatten had wanted – except that there was none of the quiet happiness he had hoped for: the manner of his death had precluded that feeling.

Andrew took part not only in the commemoration of a relative who had had great influence in the family, he took part in probably the last great public occasion which recalled the sacrifices and heroism of the British nation which had brought it victory in the Second World War.

It was an occasion that would remind him all his life of the traditions of a nation which he had been called by birth to serve. It was, in fact, only a few days later – 12 September – that he reported to the Royal Naval College at Dartmouth to begin his training in the service to which so many of his family, including Lord Mountbatten, had been proud to belong.

Another chapter in Andrew's life was beginning.

This photograph of the three Princes was taken at Balmoral in the summer of 1979. Charles was thirty-one, Andrew was nineteen, and Edward fifteen.

IO

Taking Wing

Prince Andrew Mountbatten-Windsor was twenty on 19 February 1980, but there is still much for him to experience before his character is finally moulded. But it is fair to say that, unlike his brother Prince Charles, he has developed early and seized life with both hands with energy and determination.

He is the second son of the Queen, but by his every action is intent on showing to the world that there is nothing second-rate about him. It is as if he looks at life, with the eye of an ancestral Plantagenet prince, as a battlefield to master.

He searches for challenges to prove himself – on the playing-field, in gliding, sailing, parachuting and flying and now in training to be a helicopter pilot with the Royal Navy. He is intelligent, charming at will, aggressive when necessary to get his way. Handsome in a rugged way, he is attractive to girls, knows it and has needed their company since adolescence as a foil to the male world against which he pits himself.

Certainly he is such a prince as the British royal family has not produced for a very long time. Sometimes he seems to resemble one of the younger sons of George III – courageous and self-willed – but he has shown no sign yet of their self-indulgence. He can be as charming as the Stuarts (always excepting James II), but seems fortunately to lack their deviousness. Given the power, Andrew might have developed the statecraft and ruthlessness of a Tudor. But it is as a warrior prince that it is easiest to class him.

But all this inheritance comes from his mother's side; perhaps the truth is that the Mountbatten blood of his father flows strongly in him. Intelligent, courageous, charming, generally endowed with good looks, the Battenberg-Mountbatten family has proved formidable, for its gifts are allied with great ambition.

Whatever influences from the past may have developed Andrew's basic characteristics it will be fascinating to see to what use he will put his energy and ambition, within the bounds of his position as the second son of a constitutional monarch.

Picture Acknowledgments

Illustrations in this book are reproduced by kind permission of the following:

HM the Queen: 9 *below*

Associated Press: 35 *above*, 73 *above left*, 83 *above*

Camera Press: 15 *above*, 19 *above right*, 27 *above right*, 27 *below left*, 29 *above left*, 35 *below left*, 39, 43, 49, 53, 56–7, 61 *above*, 65 *above*, 69 *above*, 73 *below*, 75 *above*, 77 *below right*, 79, 83 *below*, 91, 93 *below*

Central Press: 19 *below*, 33 *below*, 61 *below left*, 69 *below*, 75 *below*, 107, 113

Fox Photos: 15 *below*, 77 *above*

Popperfoto: 9 *above*, 25, 27 *below right*, 29 *below*, 31, 33 *above*, 35 *below right*, 65 *below*, 73 *above right*

Press Association: 19 *above left*, 27 *above left*, 29 *right*, 61 *below right*, 77 *below left*, 93 *above*, 95 *below*, 112, 125, 129

Index